CITY OF GOLD
AND
OTHER STORIES FROM THE
OLD TESTAMENT

CITY OF GOLD
AND
OTHER STORIES FROM THE
OLD TESTAMENT

Retold by
PETER DICKINSON

Illustrated by
MICHAEL FOREMAN

LONDON
VICTOR GOLLANCZ LTD
1980

ISBN 0 575 02883 1

Photoset in Great Britain by
Rowland Phototypesetting Ltd, Bury St Edmunds, Suffolk
and printed in Great Britain by
Westerham Press Ltd, Westerham, Kent

CONTENTS

Five: The Road to Jerusalem

Six: Princes and Prophets

Seven: The Stones of the Temple

Notes

ONE
IN THE BEGINNING

THE STORIES BEFORE HISTORY. GOD makes the world, and makes Adam and Eve to be parents of Mankind. They lose His favour, and are driven from Eden. Their children fill the world, but are almost destroyed in the Flood. Then Noah's children fill the world again.

The Fall of Man

Told in exile, in Babylon, at an open-air feast given by a Babylonian nobleman. About 575 BC.

My lord does his servant great honour, commanding his servant to speak before these lords and ladies.

A tale of my own people? And suitable for a feast in these fair gardens, which are a wonder of the world?

We have no such gardens as these, we Hebrews. We grow good grapes and olives, and famous figs, but these flower-hung terraces, these green groves—no, nothing like this. Our enemies might say that it is because at root we are still a wild people, a desert people who worship a desert God. But I would answer that we have no longing for such beauties because in our hearts there is already a garden—that first garden which God planted in a place called Eden, and which he made more beautiful even than the scented arbours in which my lord has given this noble feast.

It was not only in beauty that the Garden of Eden excelled all others. It was different in its nature. In that garden there was no death.

See, lords and ladies, there beyond the stream, where the slaves are working in the lemon-grove, hoeing out weeds, raking in the dried blood and the powdered bone of dead animals. And there, where those others are searching through the vines for caterpillars and squashing what they find between finger and thumb. In my lord's garden plant and insect and animal must die, so that his eyes may feast on beauty.

But in the garden of which my people tell, the thistle grew with the fig-tree, each in the splendour of its kind and neither the enemy of the other. The caterpillar sucked at the juices of the lily, and the lily rejoiced in giving and was not hurt. All grew in one delighting harmony. Moreover, all beasts, wild and tame, roamed through the garden at peace with each other. The lion laired with the lamb and the lamb was not afraid.

No, my lady, the lion did not eat grass—he is of too proud a kind. He ate as my lords would eat if some strong sorcery were to turn them suddenly into animals—for they too would surely all be lions, and my ladies would be gazelles. He ate nectarines, and loquats, and grapes, and the trees bowed down to give him their fruits as he paced by.

Now, in this garden, over all these plants and beasts, God had set a man—just as my lord has set a senior slave to see that all this garden is duly ordered. This man's name was Adam, and he was the only man God had made. Just as my lord is careful for the happiness of his slaves, so God was careful for Adam, and made him a wife to complete his happiness.

How did He make her, O my lady of many questions? Why, when Adam slept one night God took from him one little rib-bone—here on the left-hand side—and breathed on it and it became Eve, the mother of us all. When Adam woke in the dew of that first morning and saw her, his heart sang. They were naked in the sunrise, and felt no strangeness. Day by day they walked through the garden, rejoicing in each other and the world which God had given them.

Now I must speak of the tree, and of the serpent. In the middle of this garden, in a clear space by a stream, was a tree. No man knows its kind, but some of our scholars have written that its leaves were not green flesh but clear flame, and it was the self-same tree that Moses saw when God called him to the holy mountain. However, it is known that the tree bore fruit, for God had commanded Adam that of all the trees in the garden this was the only one whose fruit he must not eat. When first Adam showed Eve the delights of the garden he told her God's command, and the serpent, who had been secretly following them in their wanderings, heard him speak.

"Why is this so?" asked Eve.

"I do not know," said Adam.

The serpent heard this also.

This serpent was not then as he is now. He was golden-red in colour, winged like a bird, with feet like a lizard's and a crest like a king's crown. If he willed, he could breathe fire from his mouth, and he had the power of speech. Of all the animals in the garden he was nearest to Adam in wisdom, so the serpent and the man had been companions until the coming of Eve, sitting together under the stars and riddling out the wonders of God's creation.

Alas, lords and ladies. From this seed sprang all the sorrow of the world, for in his delight in his bride Adam forgot his long friendship with the serpent.

The seasons passed until a morning came when Eve, roaming alone beside the central stream, found the serpent there, gazing at its image in the water.

"What are you studying, friend?" said Eve.

"I am considering why I am as I am," said the serpent.

"That is a deep question," said Eve, and she knelt among the rushes and looked at herself in the water, and wondered.

"I shall never know," she said with a sigh.

"Only God knows, who made you," said the serpent.

"Do you think He will tell me?" said Eve.

"No," said the serpent.

She sighed again.

"If you ate the fruit of the fiery tree, you might know," said the serpent.

"Do you think so?" said Eve.

"Why else should He have forbidden it?" said the serpent.

"But He *has* forbidden it," said Eve.

"If you know what God knows you will be equal with Him, and He will have no power over you," said the serpent.

Then Eve went to the tree and picked one fruit from among the flames and bit it in half. As her teeth pierced the rind the flames died and only bare dead branches remained. The taste, lords and ladies, is still in our mouths, for it is the taste of knowledge, sweet at first, bitter at last. The serpent did not eat, because he was afraid, so Eve carried the other half of the fruit to Adam and told him how sweet the taste of it was.

"But it is forbidden," said Adam.

Then Eve repeated the serpent's arguments, cunningly hiding the lies beneath the truths because of the knowledge that was in her. So Adam believed her and ate the other half of the fruit.

Now Adam looked about him and saw the garden with the eyes of knowledge. He saw the lion stalking between the tree-trunks and knew that its talons were fashioned for striking at its prey and its mouth for the rending of flesh. He saw the lamb grazing in the glade, and he knew that its meat was juicy and tender. He saw the lion leap on the lamb and slay it.

Eve's month-old child wailed in its arbour, and when Eve went to comfort it and carried it out still wailing, Adam saw its little clenched fists striking in fury at emptiness, and knew that they would grow to be strong, clutching hands, the hands of Cain, who was first to murder a man.

Then Adam and Eve looked at each other and knew the shame of their nakedness, and hid.

That evening God came to the garden. As my lord might stroll along these terraces in the cool of dusk and see small disorders which spoilt their beauty—a mildewed rose, a hibiscus limp with drought—and call to his senior slave to account for the neglect, so God called to Adam and Eve. At last they came creeping out, trying to hide their nakedness with branches, and He knew what they had done.

"You have made your choice," He told them. "You have chosen the sweat of ploughing and the ache of reaping, the pain of childbirth and the grief of children. The knowledge you have eaten is the knowledge of death. So you have no longer any place in this garden."

He took from the serpent his royal crown and his fiery breath, his wings and his legs, and made him creep on his belly in the dust; and the companionship which once held between the man and the serpent was turned to hatred, and to this day each strikes at the other the moment they meet.

Then God opened the walls of the garden and showed Adam the wilderness of the world which he now had to cultivate and people. The animals that eat plants fled through the gap, and the animals that eat flesh came hunting after them, all slaying or being slain according to their natures. And God closed the wall behind them.

For the garden is still there, guarded by four great angels, each with a sword whose brightness is such that no eye can see beyond the dazzle of it. Only our wisest men say that one day there will come a second Adam, by whom the foolishness of the first Adam will be unravelled, and then the angels will sheathe their swords, and the wall will vanish and the garden will spread through the world.

Even now, sometimes, looking at my lord's garden here in Babylon, I dream that that time must already have begun—or perhaps God has given leave for the wind to blow here some seeds out of Eden, to show my lord that he has God's blessing for his kindness to us poor Hebrews in our exile.

CAIN AND ABEL

*Told by a nomadic herdsman at a temporary market, where nomads gather
seasonally to trade animals. Period of the Judges—about 1100 BC.*

Gently, my friend, gently! Come this way. Yes, of course you are in the right
and the fellow lies—but is your life worth as little as a lame mule? Your life, I
say! Can't you see—the fellow wears the Mark! Look now, there, when he
turns his head as he argues—above the left temple that tattooed star. You've
not seen it before? Well, you are new to these plains and if you stay you will
see it often, especially when you go south for the spring grazing. That's no
mere ornament—it is the Mark, which all his clan must wear. Come and sit
here by my tent and I will tell you the story while my daughters fetch sherbet
to cool your anger . . .

In the beginning were Adam, the Father of Mankind, and Eve his wife, and
they had sons and daughters. Now, the first son they named Cain, and when
he was a man he became the first farmer—one of that dull, settled breed who
plough their ground and sow their seed and wait for it to grow so that they
may plough and sow again, always in the same dull valley. You know the
kind, sullen with strangers, mean with hospitality, a fierce dog chained at the
doorpost—that was Cain.

But Adam's second son, whom they called Abel—he lived our life, journey-
ing between the hills and the plains as the seasons brought fresh grass for his
herds, not looking downwards all the time, like his brother spying for vermin
among the crops, but up at the stars to find his way across the trackless

17

plains, always in the hand of God, who set the stars there, who fills the wells, who provides the grazing. What Gods do farmers worship? Vile Baals, with their filthy rituals. But Abel was a man like us, open-handed, welcoming a stranger to his tent though he had to kill his last goat to feed him.

Now in those days God lived closer to man than He seems to now; when He spoke in their hearts they knew it was His voice, and when they made sacrifice He would answer—if their gifts pleased Him flame would stoop from the sky, so bright that the man must shut his eyes, and when he opened them the stone of sacrifice would be empty, and his gifts gone. So it was with Abel, who laid on the stone the finest of his flock, the first of his lambs. God was pleased and took the gift.

But Cain treated God as he treated the stranger. He laid on the stone the barley which was left over when he had filled his bins, the fruit with the worm in it, the loaf of last year's baking which had begun to mildew. God does not take such gifts. He spoke in Cain's heart, saying, "I reject your sacrifice because it is given with a grudging hand. Cain, Cain, you keep a dog chained at your door to drive away the stranger. Can you not see the beast chained at your heart, a beast which hungers not for the stranger but for you? You have reared it and fed it and can still be its master, but if you do not open your heart to me, as you should open your house to the stranger, the beast will master you."

For this Cain hated his brother, more and more each day, until one evening when he met him on the hills above the sown lands, he began to shout at him, saying, "Your thieving goats have eaten my young barley. I will see you pay for every blade."

"My herds have been over beyond the range for thirty days," said Abel.

"Come down into the field and see," shouted Cain.

They walked down, with Cain whining and grumbling about a year's work wasted and the starvation of his children—and indeed they did come to a place where the crops had been trampled and eaten. But Abel pointed among the smashed stems to the droppings of gazelle, and then to a hoof-print. You and I know that any man who has to track strayed animals must be able to read such signs, but by then Cain was too mad with his rage to see them. Instead, as Abel was kneeling to point out a place where the marks were very clear, Cain swung his staff and struck him on the nape of the neck and killed him with a blow.

Then, then he was afraid. He fetched a mattock from his shed and dug a pit and rolled the body into it and piled stones above it and covered them with earth, to hide what he had done. But as he walked home God spoke in his heart, saying, "Cain, where is your brother? He has made Me no sacrifice this evening."

"How should I know where he is?" snarled Cain. "He is a feckless, unreliable wanderer. Am I the herdsman's herdsman, to bring him back when he strays?"

"Cain," answered God, "the seeds you sow spring to life at My command and the earth feeds them through My power. Now they cry to Me—blade and clod and your brother's blood crying from the field where you killed him. Blade and clod will serve you no more, Cain."

"You always favoured him, never me," said Cain.

"You chose that it should be so," said God. "Now you have chosen again. You have made it impossible for blade and clod to serve you. You will have to become a wanderer, looking for food wherever I may cause it to be."

"How can I live that life?" wailed Cain. "I have never welcomed the stranger, so why should he welcome me? Every man's hand will be against me. He will remember what I did to Abel, and strike and slay me too."

Then God in His mercy reached down from the sky and the forefinger of His hand touched Cain on the temple and made a burning star. And God put into all men's hearts the knowledge that whoever struck or wounded Cain would suffer the vengeance of God, seven blows for each blow, seven wounds for each wound. So Cain went forth in safety to the empty desert to wander there with his family all his life.

God's mercy is on his family still, though the clans descended from Cain are never many; but when they come to manhood their mothers mark their temples with a tattooed star, as a warning to the rest of us. That fellow there who sold you the lame mule and swore it was sound is one of them. They do not live by our rules.

Listen, suppose I were to kill you by treachery, your cousins would hunt me out and kill me, and that would be just. But suppose I killed you in a fight which you had begun, or suppose my donkey were to kick out as we sat here and accidentally crack your skull, then I would pay the blood-price and either your brothers would be satisfied or else the elders of our two clans would meet and argue the matter out. Yes?

But it is not so with the sons of Cain. For them blood cries out and can only be answered by blood. If you had struck that fellow, as he well deserved, he would have drawn his knife on you. Then you would have drawn yours and fought, and perhaps won. Then, though all of us who stood by might have sworn that he was more to blame than you, his cousins would have tracked you down and killed you. Though you had fled beyond the mountains,

into the cities by the sea, they would still have followed you. They are like the wild red dogs of the east, who never leave the trail.

You will remember this story? If you can help it, have no dealings at all with men who wear the Mark. If you must speak with them, keep your voice low and your temper even. Your life is worth more than a lame mule, surely.

Talking of which, my wife's cousin died as we came south; no, no condolences—he was an old man and ready to die. But he rode a good sound mule which I now have no use for, and if you would still be interested—you wouldn't be throwing good money after bad, I can promise you—I do not wear the Mark—I cannot afford quarrels . . .

THE FLOOD

Told during the exile by a professional Hebrew entertainer, comparing notes with a Babylonian rival. About 550 BC.

Strange! So like and yet so different! These squabbling gods of yours! Destroying all mankind as if for a whim, too. And your hero winning everlasting life at the end. Well, I suppose my people tend to expect less of their heroes and more of their God. Yes, that's where the heart of the difference lies, I think. The details may echo each other—the animals, the boat, the bird sent forth—but your Utnapanishtim is a king and a hero who becomes a kind of god, while our Noah is never more than a mere man. But our God . . . He breathes through all our stories . . . He is their weather and landscape . . . the One God, without shape or particular dwelling. He made all things, and loves what He made as a stern father loves his children, rewarding where reward is due, but punishing even to death for error.

Now I will begin. I will spare you the music, my friend—my boy is tired, and I must have him alert for the Princess's banquet tomorrow. There is not much music in any case—a zither for the rain and a loose drum for the thunder. Let me fill your cup. Now . . .

Long ago, when the world was newly made and the servants of God were resting from their toil around the throne, they looked down from the sky. Then on the fields of earth they saw the daughters of men, walking in the beauty God had given them. Because of their loveliness the servants of God forgot their duty about the throne, and stole down from heaven and appeared to the daughters of men as warriors and kings of irresistible wealth and splendour, and the daughters of men took them for lovers.

So in due season it came about that strange beings were born in the houses of men, babes who spoke with mysterious knowledge from the moment they were born and grew to become fierce heroes and terrible giants and women with magical powers. These creatures, belonging neither to earth nor to heaven, but with each part of their nature corrupting the other, mingled among mankind and corrupted them too. Soon men began to forget the God who had made them, and tried to make these creatures into gods, worshipping them with rituals of lust and torture, each generation of men corrupting the next into yet greater vileness.

For a while God stayed his hand, but there came a generation when He saw that unless He cleansed the world of its sickness there would be no life left that was not diseased beyond cure. Still in His mercy He waited. At last there was just one man in all the world who remembered the true worship of God, and kept faith with man, and guarded his children against corruption. Noah was his name.

In a dream that was not a dream God spoke to Noah and showed him a ship, riding on stormy waters. It had neither mast nor sail nor rudder, but a full two hundred paces was its length, and thirty paces its breadth, and it was taller than the tallest cedar. One great door opened in its side, and a little window in its roof, and it was all black with tar.

"This you must build," said God.

Noah woke, and prayed and gave thanks. Then he sent for his sons and they pulled down all his barns, saving the timber. He took money, all that he had, and bought more timber, and pitch, and canvas. He hired carpenters and paced out the ground and told them what they must build. So Noah made the boat God had showed him, a wonder of the world, standing black on the bare fields where his crops had grown.

Now God spoke in the hearts of all the animals of the world, according to their capacities. Two of every kind He chose, male and female, perfect, without scar or sore, and they gathered towards the fields of Noah, creeping, flying, running, or burrowing through the earth. In the day and hour when the last peg was driven home they marched, orderly as a king's army, up the ramp and through the great door in the side of the boat. And God restored to them the condition of Eden so that the beasts of prey could eat the fodder which the sons of Noah had stored in the boat.

In the day and hour (*the boy starts the drum now*), in the day and hour when the last animal passed the door, and Noah and his family drew up the ramp to close it, God loosed the rain. And more than rain. He loosed the under seas upon the land. For you must know that above the sky are waters and below the earth are waters, and only the strong hand of God holds them apart so that His world may live between. For His cleansing of that world He loosed His hold and the blue waters of the sky came streaming down and the black waters of the abyss came roaring up and the world was drowned. Then died the giants and the heroes and the women skilled in sorcery. Then died the corrupted men—and the corrupted beasts also, the winged lions and the sphinxes, the dragons and the unicorns, and none was ever seen again.

Only the boat which Noah had built floated on the water, a huge black coffin containing all the life that lived. In that darkness Noah prayed and gave thanks, and all the creatures with him prayed and gave thanks also, according to their capacities.

For forty full days and forty full nights—and the nights were no blacker than the days—they listened to the boom of rain upon the roof and the roar and suck of waves against the hull. But at last the noises ceased, as God stilled the storm and commanded the waters to withdraw to their ancient places. For another twenty days Noah waited, and then he opened the little window which God had shown him he must make in the roof and cast one of the ravens up into the sky. The bird rose, croaking with the shock of light. Noah watched it circle, fly east, fly west, and settle back to his hand, so he knew that there was no land yet to be seen.

Seven days later he took one of the pigeons and cast it up, watching it spiral into the blue of noon, but then like the raven it circled back down to his hand.

Seven days later still, he took the other pigeon and cast it up. It rose circling as before, and then with a slap of wings sped eastwards, out of sight. He waited at the window until the sun was low, and there, gliding out of the dusk, was his pigeon. When it settled onto his hand he saw that it had gathered material for a nest, a twig of fresh olive with the leaf-buds just breaking into silver, so he knew that somewhere the land was dry.

Seven days later still he cast the same pigeon out and this time it did not return.

Next morning Noah and his sons let down the ramp and gazed from the sill of the door to see where the storm had blown them. The keel had come to rest on the great mountain Ararat in the far north. Far down in all the valleys gleamed the still-receding waters, half-veiled by mist where the slopes of the mountain steamed under God's strong sun, but at their feet the grass-blades were succulent with quick growth.

God spoke His word again in the hearts of all the animals so that they came

marching out, orderly as a king's army, and began to scatter along the range seeking new lairs and new pastures. A soft wind blew the last of the storm-clouds westward and as Noah gazed he saw a shining arch of many colours building itself against the blackness of the cloud.

Once more God spoke in Noah's heart.

"This is My sign, My promise. Never again will I loose the waters to cleanse the world, but from this day on season will follow season and harvest harvest, all in their true order."

So Noah gazed at the shining arch, and the cleanness of the world which God had given back to him, and he and all his family prayed and gave thanks.

You see? Very like, but very different. Oh no! Yours is a fine story, with its great clashing lines. No wonder you need nine musicians to do it justice—and there are one or two details I think I shall steal, next time I tell mine . . . Alas, I cannot take your gods very seriously . . . Now, more wine and then what? Three gods who appear to an old childless couple who entertain them, not knowing who they are? And are rewarded with a son in their old age? Yes, I have one something like that. Roll the dice again and we will see who tells his tale first . . .

Babel

Told by an old man to calm his grandchild, who has been frightened by a troop of ecstatic prophets passing through the village. Time of the Judges, about 1100 BC.

What is the matter, little plum? Wild men in the road, naked and screaming? So you came to your old grandfather and woke him up, because you were afraid? It's all right—I'd finished my nap—I'm not angry. Find my stick, little plum, and help me from the ground . . . there. Now hold me by the hand in case I fall down, and take me out and show me these wild men . . .

How they leap! What a noise of tambourines! It makes me glad I'm a little deaf, almost. Run and beg a few cakes from your mother—tell her it's for the prophets, so that they may bless us . . .

Now take your cakes to that man with the red staff. Don't be frightened— they've stopped jumping about. Ask him to bless your father's household . . .

Well done! And he blessed you? What's that? You couldn't understand the words, but he smiled? Then I think we may take it that he did bless you . . .

What's that again? Speak slower and louder, little one. Why couldn't you understand the words? Well, it's an old story—are you too busy to listen to a story? Then come and sit by me here and I will tell you.

Once upon a time, long long ago, soon after Noah and his flood, there were still not many men in the world so they all lived as one tribe, moving with their flocks, all together, from place to place. And of course they all spoke one language—the same language that Adam spoke with God in the Garden of Eden. It isn't like that now, little plum. You know that if you went south for many days you would meet a people who spoke words which had no meaning for you, because you would be in Egypt, where they speak Egyptian? The same if you went east to the Ammonites, or north to the Phoenicians. And few of them would understand your Hebrew. Things were easier in those old days. All men spoke the same language, and praised God with it.

Now these men I told you about, they wandered east, into the land of Shinar, until they came to a rich plain in the middle of which was a mighty river. Along the banks of this river they found good clay, and near by a pool of black tar—yes, just like your father uses to paint a wound on one of his sheep, where the maggots have broken the skin—but think, not a little pot of the stuff but a great, black, sticky pool of it.

In the land of Shinar there is little rain, and these men found that they only had to dig clay from the river bank and shape it into blocks and set it to dry in the sun, and they had good strong bricks. Then they found that if they set one brick on another with a smear of tar between, the bricks would stick together. So with bricks and tar they built themselves houses—the first houses ever— and praised God. They built a village—the first village ever—and thought how clever they were and praised God. They built a wall round the village and called it a city—the first city ever—and marvelled at their own cleverness. But in their marvelling they forgot to praise God.

Now they were in the habit of building. When they had finished their city they began to build a tower—the first tower ever. They wanted to show there was nothing they could not do. Never was such a tower! Day after day it grew, as they brought their bricks and tar and laid them together, toiling like ants going into a nest with grass-seeds, each man with his load. The tower grew taller than their houses, taller than the city wall, taller than the tallest tree, taller than the hills they had left behind! At sunrise and sunset its shadow stretched across the plain a full day's march. If a cloud crossed the sky, its skirt trailed in mist over the workmen at the top. They began to feel that the sun and the stars were very near.

All this while God had been watching the doings of His men. They might have forgotten to praise Him—they were too busy praising themselves—but He had not forgotten them. Of course, He could easily have sent an earthquake or a wind and simply tossed their tower down as you might toss down a little straw hut you have built for your doll, but He knew men. They would have quarrelled for a while, each calling the others fools for not building the tower strong enough, and then they would have started again.

No, God doesn't work like that. Instead He came down and walked invisibly among the builders, and as He passed each man He breathed into each

mind a little word, a different word for each mind. Each word was a seed. From it grew a whole language, a different language for each man. So when that man next straightened from his task to call for more tar, or a special shape of brick, or a level or a plumb-line, the others stared at him with their mouths open, as if he had gone mad. Soon they were all gaping and running about like ants when you break into a nest, not one of them understanding any of the others but each making perfect sense to himself.

For a few more weeks they went on building, trying to use signs, or drawings in the mud; but their minds had all grown different and they could no longer work to one end. The tower grew and grew, but now it grew crooked, and the men looked at it and tried to explain to each other what was wrong, but that was no use. Then, in the dark of one night God told a mouse to go and burrow under the foundations at a corner of the tower. Do you know, the work of that one mouse was enough to make the tower begin to tremble?

And soon it was rocking, and now the whole plain was shaking, and great cracks opened in the walls of the houses, so that the men and their families got up and ran out into the shaking plain. As the sun came up the foundations at last gave way. That tower fell, clean across the city from wall to wall, smashing houses, temples and shops, in a great pink cloud of brick-dust.

When the wind had blown the dust away there was nothing to see but a mound of rubble where the city had been, and the broken stub of the tower. If you travel to the land of Shinar, even now, you may still see it, and guess how huge the whole tower must have been. But the men could no longer live together so they set out on their travels, each with his family, speaking his new language, and they became the fathers of all the nations on earth today.

The wild men, little plum? The prophets? I forgot. Yes. I don't know what the priests say, but what my father told me is this. God made man to praise Him, and gave him a language for that praise. But when we built the tower He took the language away and left us to praise Him as best we can in our own languages. Still from time to time He chooses men to praise Him in the old way, and touches their minds so that they can speak the true language. But these words are so strong—they are like wine to a man who has long drunk only water—that our minds can scarcely bear them, and we throw off our clothes and leap and shout as though we were drunk or mad, and nobody can understand us, nor we each other. Nor can we remember what we said or meant, when God has withdrawn His power.

But think, little plum, what a strong blessing a blessing in that language must be. So go and tell your mother what happened, and thank her for the cakes, while I sit here in the sun and have another nap.

TWO

THE PROMISE TO THE FATHERS

THE START OF JEWISH HISTORY—
about 2000–1600 BC. Abraham migrates
into Canaan, and God promises him His
special favour, and gives him the land for
his descendants. The promises are renewed for his
son Isaac, and then for his grandson, Jacob. But in
time of famine Jacob and his sons migrate into Egypt.

SODOM

Told by a priest of the Temple, talking to a colleague during the siege
shortly before the fall of Jerusalem. 587 BC.

———◆———

. . . but all my long life I have served Him here in His Temple. I have kept not
only the Laws but all the trivial Rules. Now the armies of the heathen camp
round our walls. My children's children starve in their cots. Why does He
send me such dreams? See if you can interpret them for me.

I had been reading in the Great Scroll of Abraham about the destruction of
Sodom, and last night I dreamed that I saw all that I had read. It was the same
as in the scroll, but at the same time new-seeming, full of mysteries, but more
real than dreams should be. Do you remember ever dreaming of odours? Nor
do I, and yet the stink of sulphur is still in my nostrils.

You will remember in the scroll God and two others came to Abraham and
told him that Sara, barren till now, would have a son who would father a
great nation. And then that God told him also that Sodom was doomed to
destruction for its wickedness, and that Abraham begged God to spare the
city for the sake of his cousin Lot, who lived there, and that God sent His two
companions to tell Lot to leave and never look back? All that, after a fashion, I
saw in my dream.

First I was in a wide plain below a range of hills. It was near sunset. Flocks
of nomadic herders moved homeward in clouds of golden dust. I came close
to the hills and saw tents pitched under a grove of wide-topped, twisted
trees. A man sat at the entrance to the largest tent, bearded, dark-featured,

very still, with that hooded look you see in the eyes of men who are used to the desert. I knew this was Abraham.

Now from the south came men, three of them, not walking but gliding at great speed a little above the ground. Though their faces were towards me, I could see no features, not even eyes, but Abraham rose and greeted them without surprise, only with that deep formality desert people show to their guests. Sara, old and scrawny, brought food from the tent. The strangers ate while Abraham watched. When they talked I could hear their voices but not the words, though now I seemed to stand quite near. I longed to hear, for at that moment, surely, God was making the Great Promise to Abraham, which was also the Promise to us, that His favour was on us, and that all this land would be ours for ever.

Only, suddenly, in the tent, I heard Sara laugh—laugh at the thought that in her old age she should bear a son to become the father of nations. That was all I heard of the Great Promise.

Now, as happens in dreams, the three strangers and Abraham were gliding fast as cloud-shadow up the hill behind the tents. On the topmost ridge they stopped and looked east. Below lay the Salt Sea, very blue, as I have seen it from that self-same ridge—only all round it lay not sun-battered desert but a smooth plain, soft and green as the sea-coast of Lebanon. A gentle haze softened the sun and hid the distances, but even so I could see the towers of two fine cities floating between the fields and the water. The sea was flecked with the sails of their boats and the dust of many carts rose round their gateways.

Now I saw Abraham was kneeling before the tallest of the strangers, who had become not a man but a column of golden brightness from which a voice came, and yet it was not a voice. It was thunder shaped into syllables, decreeing the doom of the cities. But I understood Abraham now, speaking plain Hebrew, begging that the good should not perish with the wicked. The thunder answered and he beat his head on the ground and gave thanks.

Then again all shifted. The two companions of God were gliding down the far slopes of the range with myself invisible beside them. I knew that we were moving towards places of vile works and viler worship, and I was afraid, but at the same time tingling with excitement, a longing to see the wickedness, to gaze into the face of absolute evil before it was destroyed. I was sure that what was utterly forbidden must also be utterly beautiful.

Next, abruptly, we were at the gate of a city. Now the dream-like gliding was forgotten and all felt real and ordinary, except that still no one seemed able to see me, though my limbs were sore with long travel and I was covered all over with sweat and the clogging road-dust. The guards at the gate questioned the two strangers but not me. People went by. They did not have wickedness stamped on their faces, only that withdrawn and hurrying look you used to see on market days here in Jerusalem before the siege. Still I was sure those faces were masks which had only to slip or melt and then I would see the devil-leer that betrayed the secret soul.

A man rose from beside the gate and spoke to the guards, saying that he would vouch for the strangers. With my dream-knowledge I knew that this was Abraham's nephew Lot. He led them away. As I hurried behind I remembered from the scroll what would happen next—the people of Sodom would gather and demand to be given the strangers, so that they could do vile things to them. But despite my fear, I peered this way and that among the tall houses. I peeped through doorways and into barred windows, hoping to glimpse abominable rites, naked couplings on the altars of sneering idols, but I saw only the distant flicker of lamps, and heard faint music or laughter from far chambers.

Now we were inside Lot's house. His daughters brought a meal for the strangers. They seemed able to see me, and I ate too. All was quite ordinary. Then I was aware that the lamp-flicker I had glimpsed in the secret houses had drawn close around this house, and that the laughter had become the shrieking of carrion birds. I looked from a window and saw a crowd of citizens, their faces earnest under the torchlight, calling to Lot to say who his guests were, shouting that there was a rumour of spies in the city. Before anyone could answer the crowd had changed. They were human still, but screaming like madmen, yelling for death to all foreigners. They changed again. The masks melted and I saw the devil-faces I had imagined, slavering for rape and torture.

All at once I myself was out in the street, in the thick of the crowd, terrified that I might be recognised for a stranger, but at the same time screaming with the rest against these spies, these desert bandits. I saw one of Lot's guests appear at a window and hold up a shining hand, so bright that I screwed up my eyes. When I opened them the street was filled with a strange darkness, thick and fluffy, like soot. I stumbled about in the blackness trying to find the door, but met only other gropers and stumblers. Hands brushed my face, seemed to feel for my throat . . .

I woke, rigid, as one does from a nightmare. I heard the cry of a sentry, was aware of the comfort of my own room and of the hunger in my stomach, and then I was back in my dream. I stumbled down a dreary track across a vast plain strewn with glittering boulders of salt. All sense of gliding was gone.

My limbs were so heavy I could barely move them. Far ahead of me walked Lot, with his wife beside him. Their shoulders were bowed and they moved with a hopeless automatic trudge, such as we saw here in Jerusalem when the country people streamed in through the gates while the armies of Babylon gathered from the north.

I too trudged that hellish path. The clouds above were sagging black, but lit on the underfolds with an orange glow, like sunset. The same light began to gleam on the cloaks of the two who walked ahead of me, brighter and brighter at each step. The whole plain trembled. Cracks opened across the path and from them rose stinking yellow smoke. The world groaned—the groan of a sleepless man remembering old wrongs that cannot be undone. I fought to catch up with the other two, to remind them of God's command that they should not look back to see the fire of heaven devouring the cities. I heaved each foot from the ground with huge effort. Just as I had almost reached them the woman turned.

It was the face of Lot's wife—but now it was my own daughter—my mother—Eve, the mother of us all—a face of ivory, its mouth opening to say the one word I must hear . . . the glare of destruction became the lightning of God and bathed her round . . .

When I opened my eyes the glare was still there, but gathered into a glistening column of the same salt rock that strewed the plain. I stared at it, searching for some feature of the woman it had been, but could see none. Far ahead Lot trudged across the plain as if unaware that his wife had vanished from his side.

Two veiled young women sauntered by me, untroubled and murmuring in low tones. I knew them for Lot's daughters. I had seen them in his house, but I do not remember dreaming that part of the scroll in which Lot had offered them to the crowd in exchange for the lives of his guests. Now they stopped and looked at the white pillar. One spoke a few quiet words. Each put up a hand as if to remove her veil, but instead they stripped away the whole mask, the soft unpainted brow, the demure glance. For a moment I glimpsed that beauty I had hoped to see in Sodom, that vileness which is utterly forbidden and therefore is utterly beautiful, as they signalled to each other with all-knowing eyes. Their gaze sought out and fixed upon the distant figure of their father. They fastened masks and veils back into place and followed him.

That is all I remember. What does it mean, my friend? What does it mean for Jerusalem?

JACOB AT BETHEL

*Told by a father to his son while they are trying to catch a stray goat in
the desert beyond Jordan. Period of the Kings, about 800 BC.*

Stop! Stand still! Don't look round! Stand still, I say! Good. Now take your
sandals off and hold them in your left hand. Do as I say, boy! Now start
walking backwards towards me, still not looking round—I'll tell you if you're
going to bump into anything . . . one more step. There! Take my hand and
we'll go on walking backwards together . . . that's far enough, I should
think. Don't worry about the goat. Look, he's stopped to graze . . . perhaps
that's a sign . . .

Can you feel nothing? No strangeness? No difference? That tall rock there,
with the slab beside it? No, it doesn't matter, there's nothing wrong with you.
I heard a prophet say once that to a child all the world is holy, so how should
you feel that one place might be holier than another?

But this place is holy . . . I cannot tell you how I know, but the moment I
came up the slope and saw you there, so close to the tall stone, I knew. I
was . . . *afraid* is not the right word for it, though it is very like fear. Not like
the fear of a wild beast or the fear of battle, nor even like the terror of a
nightmare. But something like the fear of falling—when you stand at a cliff-
top, quite safe, with firm rock under your feet and your hand gripping a
tree-root, and the dread of the drop seems to tug at your mind, and your
palms chill with sweat. A little like that.

The place is holy because of that stone. There are places where He has

37

been, and He leaves part of His presence there . . . I don't know how to say it . . . You remember, two days back, when we'd just pitched camp and you called me up the hillside to show me a circle of bare ground in the grass and asked what it meant?

That's right. Men had been and made a fire, three or four months ago. We could see no men on all the hills, but by the circle of their fire we knew they had been there. It is the same where God has been—only long after He has gone His fire can still burn.

You can feel a little of it now? Good. It is important to know the feeling, in case you stumble on another place like this, out here in the wild lands. Beyond the river it is different—all the places are known, I think. They have names, and there are shrines there. It is strange to think that even a great shrine like Bethel, where all the tribes gather for the festivals, was once an empty place with a tall stone, like this.

Tell me the names of the Three Fathers. Abraham, Isaac, Jacob, that's right. And do you remember that Jacob went on a journey, when he was a young man, to find a wife? Yes, her name was Rachel, but he came to Bethel before he found her. I think perhaps he may have lost his way on his journey—there were fewer tracks then and all the land was wilder. Night fell as he was travelling, so he camped where he was, not seeing because of his weariness and the dark that the place he had chosen was different from other places. But the blessing of God was on him, and as he slept God showed him the truth. That place, which to the unbeliever might look like any other bit of wild land, with its scrub and boulders, to the seeing eye was one of those special places which God uses in His comings and goings—a place of dread and of wonder.

In his dream Jacob saw what men do not see, the long ramp that leads from earth to heaven, and Powers and Presences moving up and down it, without limbs or faces—wings of fire, voiceless singing, the servants of God.

In his dream Jacob heard God speak from among the singing flames, telling him that he was blessed, that the blessing would continue with his children and his children's children through endless generations, and that all the land of Canaan would be theirs for ever.

That blessing is still on me and on you, my son—provided we remember to listen for His voice and to obey His laws. It makes no difference that we are poor herdsmen grazing our goats in the wild lands. In some ways it is easier for us. In the towns and farms beyond the river they forget. They begin to worship vile and foolish Gods, and to measure their blessings in money, and houses, and servants, and rich clothes. Even at the shrines—yes, even at Bethel—there are the merchants' stalls and the money-changers and the

officials demanding dues. The whole place is so smothered with people and possessions that when I have gone to Bethel I have never felt what I feel here.

But Jacob felt it. He knew it. When he woke in the dawn his mind was ringing with his dream and he had no need to look around him to know where he had slept. He was filled with fear and glory, each feeding the other. He had slept with his head on a long boulder, and now God gave him the strength to heave it upright so that it stood like that one there. He blessed the stone with a sacrifice, pouring a little oil on it—that was all he had with him. He gave the place its name—Bethel, the House of God. I will take you there for the spring festival and show you the very stone—though not before we have paid our dues to the priests.

Now what must we do? Yes, a sacrifice. No, not the goat, supposing we can catch him—he won't do—he's still blotched with last year's mange. Let's see what your aunt has packed for our meal. . . Look, five little cakes. Oil. Cheese. That looks the best of the cakes. You take it and I will carry the oil. We'll leave our sandals here. They're beginning to say in the towns that only priests are allowed to make the sacrifices, but was Jacob a priest? Now, do what I do. Say what I say, and we will ask God to renew the blessing He gave to Jacob.

After that perhaps He will help us to catch the old goat.

Hungry? So am I, but . . . You're thinking about the cake we left by the great stone, uh? Try not to. It's no use giving things to God if you secretly grudge the gift. He knows all your secrets. And it's no use giving Him just what you can spare, the left-overs of your meal, the weakling kid that would have died in any case. You must give the fresh-baked loaf, the first-born kid—after all, didn't He give them to you in the first place? He gave you everything you have. The air you breathe, the water you drink, are not yours by right. They are His gift. To show that you understand this you give Him back the very best you can . . . You can't remember the last great drought . . . We were sweeping the grain-pits and sieving the dust for the last few ears we might have missed, but even from those we baked a little loaf for the altar. To make the milk to suckle you your mother was eating wild roots I dug from the hillside. Ah, that was hunger. Try not to think about the cake and I will tell you a story.

Who was Jacob's father? . . . And Isaac's? Good. This is a story about Abraham and Isaac. It may seem very strange and terrible at first, but you mustn't be afraid, because God will bring it right in the end.

Abraham lived like us, in tents, moving from place to place with the seasons to find grazing for his herds. One evening he was sitting in front of his tent when the voice of God spoke to him. God often spoke to Abraham, always with promises and blessings, but now He spoke otherwise.

"Abraham," He said, "take your son Isaac down to the country of Moriah in the south. I will show you a mountain, and a special place on the mountain where you must build a fire and make a sacrifice to me. The sacrifice will be your son, your only son, Isaac. I gave him to you as a gift in your old age, and now the time is come to give him back."

Abraham bowed his head to the dust but he did not curse or weep. All night he lay sleepless, with grief for his son struggling against his trust in God. In the morning he told his household that he and Isaac were going south to make a sacrifice, and he had his donkey saddled and told two servants to load a mule with firewood, and the four men and the two animals set out.

Two nights they spent on the way, and still Abraham told none of them what he knew, bearing his horror and his grief in silence. On the third morning he saw the mountain. He knew it at once, though it was only part of a range of hills. Perhaps it was just as I knew that stone this morning among all the other stones of the desert . . . but the mountain called to him, saying "Come!"

At the foot of the mountain he told the servants to wait with the animals. Isaac was a strong lad, older than you, so they roped the basket of logs to his shoulders and he and Abraham started to climb. Of course Isaac had been with his father to high places before and made sacrifices to God there, but still he was surprised.

"Father," he said after a while.

"Yes," said Abraham.

"You have the sacred knife, and the lamp to start the fire. I am carrying the firewood. But where is the animal to sacrifice?"

"God has given it to me," said Abraham. "It will be there when we are."

Isaac knew that his father lived very close to God, so he climbed on with no more questions.

At the top of the mountain, at the northern end of the ridge, they found a great flat stone, and at once Abraham knew it to be the place. He took the wood from Isaac and built the fire and then, using the rope with which Isaac had carried the basket up the mountain, he bound his son hand and foot and laid him on the wood. Neither of them said a word. God was on the mountain, and all around them. The dread of His presence filled their veins, but He gave no sign.

Abraham picked up the knife and looked in his son's eyes for the last time. He steadied his hand for a smooth, firm stroke at the throat which would loose the blood gushing onto the stone.

Then God spoke.

"Put down the knife. Untie the boy. You have passed the test."

Still without a word Abraham did what he was told. As Isaac rose from the stone the silence was broken by a rattling, and they looked and saw a wild sheep struggling on the slope a little below them with the curl of its horn hooked into the fork of a thorn-branch. They went down and lifted it free and found that it was a year-old ram, without scar or blotch. So Abraham bound it with the rope and laid it on the timber and gave thanks to God as he loosed its blood upon the rock.

Do you know where that rock is? Yes, but where is Moriah? I have heard several claims, but now everyone is beginning to say that they have found the place, and it is the very rock upon which King Solomon built his great Temple at Jerusalem. They're beginning to say that we must stop going to Bethel for the festivals and go to Jerusalem instead . . .

Yes, perhaps. I do not like Bethel. If your uncles agree . . . And then we shall see that golden roof, and know that underneath it, underneath the holiest room of all, lies the very rock where the blood of the ram poured out while God promised Abraham that all Canaan would belong to his children.

The great drought had not ended when you were born. Most of my lambs were born dead that spring, and the rest were too weak to walk. But I chose the strongest, and tethered its mother on the best grazing I could find and drove the other ewes off, so that at least she should produce enough milk to feed it. Then I had one fat lamb ready when I heard your wail from the women's tent, and your aunt brought you out and showed me that you were a boy, my first-born, my gift from God. For Abraham's sake, and for the sake of the promise, I sacrificed that lamb to God.

You see, we are founded, we Jews, on that moment when Abraham raised his knife to kill his son, and God held him back and gave him the ram instead. It lies beneath our being, in the same way that the stone lies beneath the Temple . . .

Look, there are the tents! Can you smell the fire-smoke? I hope you're still hungry, uh? And God's given you a wonderful appetite in exchange for that one small cake?

REBEKAH AT THE WELL

*A work-song, sung by women carrying water-jars up the spiral path
from a deep desert spring. Any period.*

Traveller from the west
In rich weaving dressed—
Camels at his back
Dusty from the track—
Waiting by the waters
For the city's daughters.
　　Who comes from the gate?
　　Ai! Rebekah. Ai! Brilliant eyes.

Lifting up his face
To the sky he says
"She who, when I ask
One sip from her flask,
Waters all my line—
God, make this the sign."
　　Who walks by the well?
　　Ai! Rebekah. Ai! Brilliant eyes.

"Maiden, let me dip
From your jar a sip."
"Drink, sir, as you will

While I fill and fill
Jar and jar again
For your camel-train."
    Who toils on the stair?
    Ai! Rebekah. Ai! Brilliant eyes.

Bracelets for her arm,
For her neck a charm.
"Can my beasts lie down
In this stranger town?"
"Sir, my father's store
Holds both feed and straw."
    Who runs to bring warning?
    Ai! Rebekah. Ai! Brilliant eyes.

Ere he would be fed
To his host he said
"Abraham, my lord,
Sent me far abroad
Seeking him a bride
For young Isaac's side."
    Who listens in the doorway?
    Ai! Rebekah. Ai! Brilliant eyes.

"You and he are kin.
God has sent his sign—
Shown the very one.
Now my search is done.
Silks for her I bring
And many a golden ring."
    Who climbs to her room?
    Ai! Rebekah. Ai! Brilliant eyes.

Lone and all alone
Isaac sits on stone.
From the sunset plain
Trails the camel-train—
Nearer still and near—
He beholds his dear.
    Who bows at his feet?
    Ai! Rebekah. Ai! Brilliant eyes.

JACOB AND ESAU

*Told by an Edomite hunter, from the country south of the Dead Sea, during
a hunting expedition with his young son. About 1000 BC.*

I bless my son on this day.
I mark this place with a cairn.
He has shot his first hare—
Henceforth shall his arrows fly true.
He has skinned his first hide—
His blade shall not twist in his hand.
Clear eye for the track
Swift thigh for the chase
Sure arm for the kill—
Such is my blessing.

There. That is done. Now, before we go back and tell your uncles to prepare
the feast I must show you a thing. It is a good sign that you made your kill so
close to the edge of the ranges. We'll go up to that ridge there . . .

Shade your eyes and look along my arm. See anything? Further—almost a
day's march. Trees, yes. Water? That's heat-haze, though there is a well there,
but . . . No, not tents. Those are houses. That is where *they* begin. The
people under roofs.

Now listen. Even when you are a grown man you do not go beyond this
ridge unless you have at least three companions. The land is ours, but *they*

say it is theirs, and if they find you there alone they will kill you. You see, they are afraid of us—and no wonder. We have given them cause!

It began in the time of Isaac. Remember Abraham, Father of the Nations? His son was Isaac, and when Isaac took a wife she bore him twin children—sons. It is said that they fought even in their mother's womb, and when they were born the younger came out clinging to the heel of the elder. So they were not born to agree. Esau, the elder, was a true man—such as you will become—strong, simple, firm to his promise, quick to anger. The other one, Jacob, was never more than half a man—soft, subtle, hiding his thoughts, biding his time. You will guess which was the father's favourite and which was the mother's.

As they grew they grew yet further apart. Esau roamed the wilderness and brought back game for the pot. Never was a hunter more skilled. But Jacob stayed by the tents, tending flocks or watching the women sow and hoe and harvest, and saying he was supervising the work. So the brothers saw little of each other, and were glad of it.

One evening, when they were no longer boys but not yet men, Esau came to the tents after a luckless day in the hills. (Remember, even the finest hunters know days like that.) He was staggering with hunger, and found Jacob stirring a pot over the fire.

"Women's work, as usual," says Esau. "I'll have some of your cooking, little sister."

"Not so fast, brother," says Jacob, smiling at the word. "What will you give me for it?"

"Anything you like," says Esau. "If I don't eat, I'll die."

"Your inheritance?" says Jacob, turning his face away and adding a finicky pinch of herbs to the pot.

"If I die it'll be yours anyway," says Esau. What did he care? There'd always be game in the hills—and Jacob was smiling for once, looking like a friend.

"I'd better have your promise," says Jacob.

So Esau laughed and gave it, and Jacob laughed with him as he poured him a plateful from the pot. It was lentils, porridge, not a shred of meat in it! Within a week Esau had forgotten—but not Jacob. Yes, it was Jacob who taught us to have long memories. We owe him that.

Well, seasons and years went by and now the boys were men, but Isaac too had grown older until he was feeble and blind, and Jacob despised him for that. But Esau remembered his father's love and care and gave it back, sitting with him in the sunset, or bringing him dishes of game and feeding him the tenderest pieces and then wiping the juices from his beard. One evening Isaac

48

said to him, "I can feel my death coming. It is time I gave you my blessing. Go hunting tomorrow, and bring back game fit for a feast of blessing, so that I can bless you with the proper ritual."

They were sitting close by the tents when he spoke, and who should be listening inside but the young men's mother? Next morning she watched Esau take his bow and lope towards the hills, then she went to find Jacob.

"Your chance is come," she says. "Kill me a tender kid and I will cook it to taste like game, and you can take it to your father and pretend to be Esau, and he will give you his blessing."

"He will know it is not Esau," says Jacob.

"I have heard you jeering at your brother, mimicking his big voice. And there's a goat-skin tanning—you can wear that and your father will feel it and think it is Esau's deer-skin cloak."

"He will curse me if he finds out," says Jacob.

"I will take the curse on me," says his mother.

So they did as the woman suggested. Imagine Isaac, waiting in the shade of a tree, feeling the chill of death in his limbs, ordering in his mind the words of the blessing he will give his son. He is blind, remember. He smells rich gravy spiced with many herbs. (They had been generous with the herbs, you can be sure—tame kid tastes of nothing compared with game.) He hears the pad of a footstep. There is something wrong with the sound, but his nostrils are full of the good smell and the saliva is busy in his mouth.

"Who's there?" he mumbles.

"Esau," says a voice. "I have food for the feast of blessing, father."

"You were quick to find game," says Isaac.

"God sent a yearling gazelle across my path," says the voice.

That is proper, thinks Isaac. *God approves of my blessing.* There is something wrong with the voice, too, but Isaac's mind is full of the blessing and the hands that place the bowl in his hands brush against him in such a way that he can feel the roughness of the hide which Esau wears in his hunting, and smell the strong reek of rough-tanned leather. Besides, the meat is good—rich-flavoured but tender for a toothless mouth. Old men think much about food, you know. They have no other pleasures left them.

The hands feed him delicately. His beard is wiped as tenderly as if a woman were doing it. His wine-cup is put into his grasp with soft care. He is pleased that Esau has smoothed his rough manners for this feast of blessing, because it shows that he understands its importance.

Now Isaac drinks from the cup and begins to speak. A father's blessing is a strong word. He calls on the fields to swell with food for this son he cannot see, the sky to loose sweet rain for him—he calls on the nations to be his slaves and his own brothers his servants. A strong word from a father about to walk into the pastures of darkness.

It is done!

Imagine again. Isaac is still sitting beneath the tree. He has slept. His stomach is full of sweet food, and his mind content with what he has done. He can feel from the warmth of the sun now striking below the branches that day is drawing to dusk. Now again he smells good food, again he calls, "Who's there?", again a voice answers, "Esau." But this time, hearing the true voice, he can recognise the falseness of the other. He begins to tremble.

"Who was here before?" he croaks. "Who brought the feast and put the cup in my hands? Who took my blessing?"

Their own thoughts answer him. *Jacob. Thief Jacob. Smiling Jacob.*

"The blessing was mine," whispers Esau.

"He has it," says Isaac. "I cannot give it again. I cannot take it back. I blessed the fields that feed him and the clouds that bring him rain. I made the nations his slaves . . . I made you his servant."

I have heard the scream of a man struck unawares between the ribs in an ambush. So Esau screamed.

"Have you nothing for me?" he cried. "Must he have everything?"

"No," sighed Isaac. "I can give you the hills. I can give you the wilderness and the animals of the wild. I can give you the great trackless sands."

He eats a little of the food which Esau has caught and cooked for him, but it has no savour. Then he blesses Esau with what there is left to bless. The sun goes down and he sits alone in the chill of nightfall, waiting to die.

That is how it began. My father told me and you will tell your children. We are the descendants of Esau, and the wilderness is ours. The people under roofs are the descendants of Jacob, and they live in the fat lands and grow rich. If you were to try to live among them you would become their servant.

But when you are a man you will go among them in another way, by night on your swiftest camel, with your brothers and cousins riding in silence beside you—and at first I shall be there too. As I have shown you the hunting of game, so I shall show you the raiding of people under roofs—the yell of attack, the roar of flame in thatch, the bellowing of panicking herds, the screams of women . . . ah, there is no game like man! And then to ride home in exultation, with glances only at the captured women and the loot loaded on captured mules—ours by right, the inheritance Jacob stole from Esau.

And all for a plate of lentil soup!

JOSEPH AND HIS BRETHREN

Told by a professional tale-teller at a wedding-feast in North Canaan
where people are jealous of the rising power of the two Joseph tribes in
the South. Period of the Judges, about 1100 BC.

Who has not heard of Jacob, master of flocks, herder of cattle, father of the Tribes?

Who does not know of the Twelve Sons of Jacob?

May today's bride bear such boys!

May they be as brave as Reuben!

May they be as handsome as Issachar!

May they be as wise as Levi!

And may they (good sirs, virtuous ladies) be as lucky as Joseph!

For Jacob, when he was old, took a new young wife (oh to be rich when one is old!) and the hussy bore him two sons to add to his ten. These were Joseph and Benjamin, and of course he doted on them, while his older sons toiled among his flocks and fought off the wild beasts and the raiders. Even when Joseph was grown enough to help with the work, did his father send him out to join the others? Oh no! His skin was too smooth for hard weather, his soul too fine for rough work. Perhaps he could come and go with orders, wearing a fine woven cloak to show that he carried his father's word.

"Water the cattle," he would tell them. "Herd the sheep to the far pastures. Cull the male kids."

"Who are you to give us orders?" they would ask.

"Aha," said Joseph. "Last night God sent me a dream. We all cut sheaves and set them in the field, and your sheaves fell down and grovelled before mine."

Fine dreams, to be sure, young Joseph had, and a fine way of reading them. It may not surprise you to learn that his brothers were not very taken with his dreams and his readings.

Now one day, when the brothers had been working long and hot in the shearing-pens, Joseph came lounging over the pastures, wearing his gaudy cloak and picking grape after grape from a bunch he carried, a bunch from Jacob's own vine. He leaned against the pen and started to tell them in his lordly, dreamy way about his latest vision—their stars and even the sun and moon paying homage to his own star.

You have shorn sheep, good sirs, and know the heat and struggle and short tempers. Will you blame the brothers that they became enraged with this dreamer, that Reuben took him by the scruff and thrust a set of shears into his hand, that Judah plucked the cloak from his slim shoulders, that Dan pushed a ram between his knees, while the rest stood and jeered at his trembling? And it wasn't long before the jeers became oaths and the oaths became blows, and then the brothers were standing in a circle, panting, staring at Joseph's body bruised and bleeding in the midst.

"He's still breathing," says Levi.

"He will tell our Father," says Judah.

"Not if we slit his throat, he won't," says Dan.

"And who will carry the blood guilt?" says Reuben. None answered that.

"Those merchants, camping last night down by West Brook," says Zebulun. "They've not left yet."

You may guess that Levi was the first to grasp at his meaning. You may even guess that poor Gad was the last. In fact he was still thinking it out when the others were on their way to sell Joseph to these merchants they'd met. They shared the price round among the ten of them, and then they bloodied and tore the famous cloak and carried it back to Jacob, saying they'd found it on the hillside with fresh lion-tracks all around it and a half-eaten bunch of grapes beside. So Jacob poured ashes on his head and mourned.

But the merchants carried Joseph into Egypt.

Egypt! Well may you sigh for wonder! There the tombs of the Kings are taller than our hills. There the river is a moving sea, and through it swim dragons. There the wheat stands high as a man and they reap it three times a year. There the chieftains eat off plates of gold and sleep in beds of ivory, and are buried all filled with spices, enough to buy a hundred pastures. That is Egypt!

And there stands young Joseph in the slave-market. The farmers and the master-builders pass him by, with barely a glance at his smooth skin and his unformed muscles. But along comes Potiphar, Captain of the Guard in the King's own palace.

"Oho!" thinks Potiphar. "I will buy this pretty boy as a toy for my pretty wife."

(Did God make any animal so stupid as a rich man with a young wife?)

Now a year passed, and another year, until seven had gone by, and the pretty boy had become a pretty man. One day he happened to be passing along by the women's quarters. (And what was he doing there? Well may you ask! But don't ask me—ask the sons of Joseph, ask among the tents of Ephraim and Manasseh!) Joseph happened, as I say, to be passing a certain door when it opened a crack, and a thin white arm snaked out and pulled him through.

Well may you purse your lips, virtuous ladies! Well may you cough and wish yourselves lucky as Joseph, good sirs! But I am not going to tell you what happened beyond that door, because as God is my witness I do not know. Ephraim will tell you, and Manasseh will swear to it, that Joseph fought like a tiger against the woman's advances, and tore himself away, leaving his loin-cloth in her grasp.

It may be so, for certainly half the household saw Joseph scuttling back to the slave-quarters with not a stitch of clothing on him. And certainly too the woman had *some* cause to be dissatisfied with the encounter, for all the household heard her at her husband's chariot-side when he rode home that evening, crying "Rape! Rape! Rape!"

Did I not tell you this Potiphar was Captain of the King's Guard? So he was, and the keys of the dungeons were his to command. You may guess it was not long before Joseph found himself in the deepest of them, as deep as the tombs of the Kings are tall.

Hidden in the darkness of the inmost earth, Joseph waited. He was not alone there, so he would talk with his companions. And what is there to do and talk about in such a place but dreaming? Now, I told you this Joseph had a fine way with dreams, so of course he set himself up as interpreter, prophesying release for one man and death for another. I do not know how many of these prophecies came true, but certainly one did, and a servant of the King was restored to favour, just as Joseph had foretold. Naturally the man was impressed by the event, and told his friends.

Good sirs, virtuous ladies! To look at the poor rags I wear you may not think that I too have lived in a palace, and told my humble tales to a King's face. Never was there such a place for rumours. One whisper that in the deepest dungeons lies a foreign wizard who can read your dreams, and all the nobles and ladies of the court are creeping down those greasy steps, with a bribe in their hand for the gaoler. But the last man to hear of the wizard would be the King.

As it happened, this King of Egypt was the first man to need him. He had been troubled by a dream both strange and strong. Night after night, scarce had he closed his eyes when he saw seven cows, marvellously fat, grazing along the pastures of the Nile. But as he stood, rejoicing at their fatness, out of the river came seven other cows, marvellously scrawny and thin, which fell on the fat cows and gobbled them up. And most marvellous of all, those scrawny monsters were not a fraction fatter when they'd done munching than when they'd begun.

Morning after morning the King would call his wizards and priests to him and tell them to read his dream. Some would say this and some say that, but he knew that none of them had read the riddle because next night he dreamed his dream unchanged. He would have their heads lopped off and send for a fresh lot of priests and wizards, day after day until he was in despair, and so were they. But then the rumour reached him that in his deepest dungeon lay a foreign wizard, a wonder at dreams. So Joseph was sent for and the King told him about the cows.

Joseph listened to the King for a while, then he closed his hearing and listened to God. At last he gathered his breath and sang:

> "Seven fat steers,
> Seven fat years.
> Plenty of meat,
> Mountains of wheat.
>
> Seven thin steers,
> Seven thin years.
> Nothing to eat,
> No flesh, no wheat.
>
> In the years of plenty
> Lay plenty aside—
> Provide, provide.
>
> Or years of famine
> Will be your reward.
> Thus saith the Lord."

That very night, for the first time since it had begun, the dream passed by the King's bed and did not trouble him. Next day he sent for Joseph again and put a gold ring on his arm as thick as my three fingers, and set him in a golden chariot, and made him his chief man over all the crops and cattle in Egypt. Joseph made those Egyptians sweat, you can be sure. He set foremen over them with whips to make them build great barns of stone, and through seven rich years he bought and stored away one half of every harvest.

Then, like a desert storm come up from nowhere, famine struck. The river refused to flood, the wheat shrivelled in the fields, the grass yellowed and died before it was tall enough for a mouse to nibble—so it was no time at all before the Egyptians were clamouring round Joseph's barns. He had bought cheap, you can guess, and now he sold dear, or he wouldn't have been Joseph. The first year they gave him their gold, the second they bartered their cattle, the third they paid with their land, and the fourth they had nothing left to give but themselves—which is why the people of Egypt are all the King's slaves to this very day!

Still the famine went on—and not only in Egypt. East to West, from the Great Twin Rivers to the sea, barely a blade grew, barely a goat grazed. But there was always food in Egypt, so nation after nation travelled down there to buy it, and Joseph took their gold. How much he put in the King's treasure-chest, and how much stuck to his own fingers, I do not know.

One day he was down at the tables where the wheat was doled out, over-seeing the work, when who should he notice among the jabbering foreigners but his own ten brothers? He knew them at once, but how should they know him—the soft-skinned boy they remembered turned into this great Egyptian lord with the gold ring on his arm and the slaves whipping the crowds to clear a path where he chose to stroll?

He smiled to himself and beckoned to his interpreter. He would not let them guess that he knew Hebrew. The savour of revenge was sweet on his lips. The interpreter called the brothers to come before Joseph.

"My Lord demands to know your nation," he said.

"We are Hebrews, ten sons of one farmer. Our crops have failed, but we have brought good gold to buy wheat."

"My Lord wishes to know whether you have any other brothers."

"Only one. We had a twelfth, but he is dead."

"My Lord says you are spies."

"No indeed! No never!"

Then the ten of them grovelled before Joseph, and he remembered his dream of the sheaves.

"My Lord says you must prove your story to him. One of you will stay here as a hostage, while the rest go back and fetch this missing brother."

At that they started to argue among themselves, for they knew that Jacob would never let Benjamin go. Joseph pretended to oversee the tables, while his ears delighted in their voices and the noise of honest Hebrew.

"It is all our fault," says Reuben. "God is punishing us for what we did to Joseph."

At the sound of his own name tears prickled in Joseph's eyes, but still he turned away and spoke to his slaves in Egyptian, giving certain orders. Next morning nine of the brothers travelled home. Their mules were laden with good Egyptian corn, but they had seen Simeon bound with ropes before their eyes and taken for a hostage.

All to no purpose. Jacob would not let Benjamin go.

But listen, good sirs, virtuous ladies! I told you that Joseph had given certain orders. When the wheat was almost gone and the brothers were emptying the last shakings from the sacks, what did they find? Why, gold! The self-same pieces they had taken to Egypt in the first place! Now, you may be sure, they were frightened. Spies, the Egyptian Lord had called them. Thieves he would say now. And all the wheat was gone and still not a blade grew in field or pasture. So they began to starve, until Jacob could bear it no longer and sent them back to Egypt, and Benjamin too, and double the weight of gold to show that they were not thieves.

Joseph had been waiting for their return, you can guess. He had set soldiers to watch the road for them, and they were seized and brought to his palace. When they saw the fierce sentries by the door they were sure it was a prison, but the Egyptian Lord greeted them with a smile. Once more they grovelled at his feet and tried to explain about the money, but he only laughed and told the interpreter to say that they had lucky faces. Then his slaves dressed them in clean linen and led them in to a great banquet, where he passed round his own gold cup, glowing with pearls, and made each one of them drink from it in turn. But that night, while they slept, once more he gave certain orders.

Next morning the brothers loaded their asses with the good Egyptian wheat and took the road. When they passed through the city gate they were still silent with the strangeness of their adventure, but as they added mile to mile they began to talk about it, and then to laugh with pleasure, and then to exult with the glory of good fortune. But now, in a silence between songs, what do they hear? Behind them on the road, a trumpet call! The bang of hooves, the clatter of chariot wheels. And now the soldiers are on them, seizing them with iron hands, tossing the sacks to the ground, emptying the good wheat onto the sand. And see, as the last ears join each pile, the glitter of gold! And on the last pile, from Benjamin's sack Joseph's own cup, glowing with pearls, from which they had drunk at last night's feast!

Once more the brothers grovel at Joseph's feet. Once more they try to tell him, through the interpreter, that they know nothing about the money.

"My Lord says he does not believe you. Nevertheless you may go, and not come back. But the one who stole his cup must stay and be his slave.

"No, no!" cries Reuben, speaking for them all. "Let any one of us stay and be his slave, but not Benjamin. My father's heart would break. Already, through our fault, he has lost his favourite son!"

"My Lord would hear more of this dead brother of yours."

Then Reuben told him the truth, as it had happened. And Joseph . . .

Good sirs, virtuous ladies, we are twelve tribes. We have our quarrels and they are often fierce. But still we are one people, and the blessing of God is on us. We are brothers, and God gave us this land to share and enjoy. Praised be His Name.

Even Joseph, looking at his brothers, hearing the story of that old fight at the shearing-pens, forgot his revenge. He wept. He sent the guards and the interpreter away and took off his tall Egyptian hat and raised them each in turn from the floor, speaking gently in Hebrew.

"Don't you know me, my brothers? Look at me. I was not always a great Lord. Long ago I was sold in an Egyptian slave-market, sold by merchants who had bought me from my brothers, brothers who had quarrelled with me at a sheep shearing. I am Joseph, and there is no blood-guilt on your heads."

Their mouths fell open. They looked at each other and back at him.

"I think he's trying to say he's Brother Joseph," said Gad at last.

Then he knew they'd understood, and all twelve laughed together so that the palace rang with the noise.

When the King heard the story he gave orders that mules should be loaded with food and wine and spices and cloths and all kinds of treasure and sent as a gift to Jacob, and then that Jacob's whole household should be brought into Egypt and given their own land, until the famine was ended. And he made the eleven brothers officers of his palace, with palaces and servants of their own. All this for Joseph's sake, because he was born lucky—which is to say the blessing of God was on him.

May the same blessing be on today's groom, and may his wife bear him sons as fine as Jacob had! And a blessing on all of you, who will spare some small gift for a poor story-teller who once told his tales in a king's palace! My thanks, virtuous lady! My thanks, good sir! . . .

THREE
OUT OF EGYPT

T HE EXODUS AND THE WANDERINGS in the desert—about 1350–1300 BC. The descendants of Jacob have become slaves to the Egyptians. Moses is told by God to lead them away. God brings plagues on the Egyptians to make Pharaoh let them go. They cross the Red Sea and come to Sinai, where God gives them the Law.

MOSES AND THE PRINCESS

Sung as a cradle-song by any Jewish mother, any time in the last three thousand years.

———◆———

Ah, ah, ah,
The soldiers came
  Hunting for the baby boy
    And his name was Moses.
His sister took him
  Hid him in the river reeds
    And his name was Moses.

Sleep, my darling,
No such soldiers here.

Ah, ah, ah,
The Princess came
  Found him in the river reeds
    And his name was Moses.
The Princess took him
  Stole away the baby boy
    And his name was Moses.

Sleep, my darling,
No such Princess here.

Ah, ah, ah,
His sister saw—
  Do you want a nurse, Princess?
    And his name was Moses.
His mother nursed him
  Never let the Princess know
    And his name was Moses.

Sleep, my darling,
Just your mother here.

THE BURNING BUSH

Told by a visiting shepherd, sitting at the camp-fire of a neighbouring tribe one night soon after the re-conquest of Canaan. About 1250 BC.

All these tales you have told are well-known, and some of them are lies. But I will tell you one you do not know, and yet it is true, for my father's father told it me, who heard it from his father, who was Caleb, the right hand of Joshua. And Joshua heard it from the lips of Moses. So listen!

It is well known how the people were slaves in Egypt, and how when we grew too many, Pharaoh King of Egypt gave orders that every man child born to the people should be killed, and it was done. And how Moses was born in the tribe of Levi, but his sister Miriam hid him under the river-bank and stole out to feed him. And how a daughter of the household of Pharaoh, an Egyptian woman, found him and took him to be her own son and schooled and fed him. All this is often told. But now I shall tell you a hidden wonder.

When Moses was almost a man he walked one day among the brickyards, where our people slaved to make the bricks from which were built the tombs of the Pharaohs, tall as mountains. He wore the dress of the household of Pharaoh, and had forgotten in his mind that he too was of our people. But his blood remembered what his mind had forgotten, as you will hear. By a stack of bricks he saw an Egyptian overseer lashing one of the slaves with a whip, just as you or I might flog a lazy donkey.

Then the blood of Moses remembered his birth. He knew that he and the slave were brothers, just as you and I are brothers for all that I come from beyond the range and wear a blanket of a different weave. He hit that over-seer with his fist and knocked him down so that his head struck a corner of the brick-stack and he died.

Days passed, and he thought the killing had not been seen. But then he came on two of our people fighting over a debt, and when he tried to settle the argument they cursed him for a murderer and asked who had made him judge over Israel. And soon after that the story of the fight began to be rumoured among the Egyptians. That was how Moses fled from Egypt into the desert and travelled down the Red Sea until he came to the Holy Moun-tain, the one that you call Horeb and we call Sinai. He did not then know that the mountain was holy, but he settled, as is well known, with Jethro the Midianite, and married one of his daughters, and herded a flock for him.

Now that is cruel country, barer than the barest hills of Canaan, as dry and hot as the plain of the Salt Lake. You and I, when our flocks have eaten a pasture bare, move on. But in the country of Midian that bare pasture would be thought good grazing. Their flocks are small and lean, and the journeys between pasture and pasture are long. So it was that Moses, looking for new grazing, brought his flock to the foothills of the Holy Mountain.

There man and beast move only when the sun is low, and in the heat of the morning they find shade and rest in it till the afternoon is half spent. Looking for such shade Moses came to a narrow cleft that seemed to lead into the heart of the mountain. It was as if a pathway had been carved towards the peaks, and this was the gateway of it. Standing like a watchman at the gate was a single tree, of a kind no man has seen elsewhere. It was half again as tall as a man, and all its branches as green as if it grew by the side of a pool, though there was nothing there for it to root into but the cracks of baked rocks. Moses walked towards it, thinking there might be water in the cleft for his sheep, but as he came near, the tree changed. Where it had been green leaves . . . look, I push this branch into the embers. See how it leaps into flame. So did the tree by the cleft become flame, bright as the sun but without smoke or crackling or any heat. Then Moses saw that the tree inside the flames was unchanged, not burning away or charring like this branch, but as green and sappy as when he had first seen it.

Now remember, this was a man who had been schooled among the wizards of Pharaoh's household, so he was used to wonders. Not at all afraid he came closer, to inspect the tree. But then a voice spoke and he knew that it was no simple wonder. The voice spoke aloud. When God speaks to man nowadays He speaks in our hearts, but this voice spoke in the ears of Moses, saying that he was standing on God's Holy Mountain. Moses came no nearer, but took

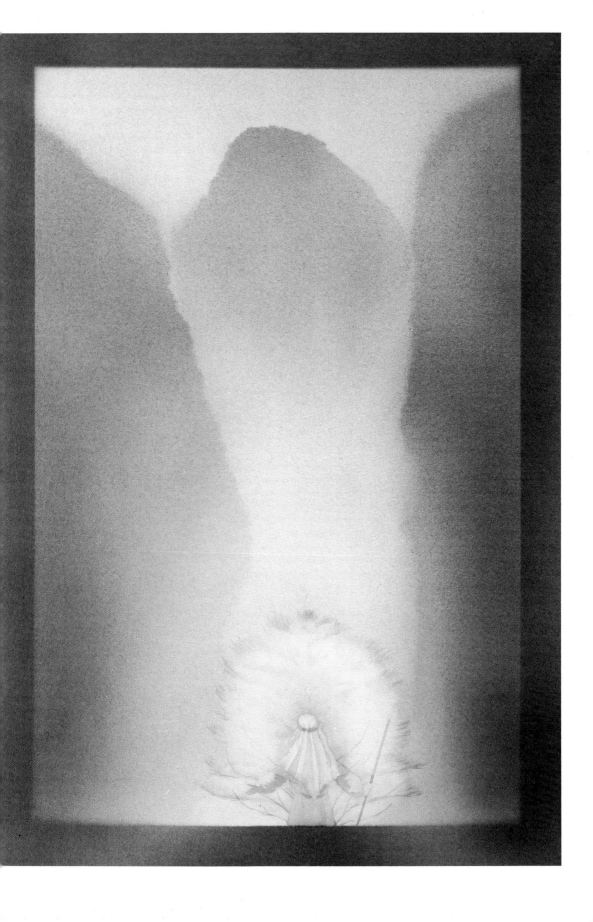

off his sandals and knelt and bowed his forehead to the ground, not bowing to the tree but to the mountain.

The voice spoke again, telling him that he must go back to Egypt, and gather the people, and bring them to the Holy Mountain to meet and worship God. Only then would they cease to be slaves, and become truly a people. All that had happened to Moses, his birth and danger and rescue, his rearing in the household of Pharaoh, the murder and the flight into the desert—all this God had willed so that he should be ready to lead the people out of Egypt.

At that Moses was afraid—the scorn of the people roared in his ears. They had cursed him for a murderer and driven him out of Egypt—what would make them listen to him if he went back?

God spoke to Moses again, a single word, the word we do not say, His own Name. He poured His power into the syllables and gave it thus to Moses. Moses rose from the ground, shuddering with the knowledge that the power was now his, that he had only to speak that Word, and the power would pour out among the people, and they would follow him.

But now a different fear smoked in his mind. He could see Pharaoh on his throne, the hard face, the cruel eyes. He could see the people toiling in the brickyards and the tomb of Pharaoh hardly begun. He could see the idle courtiers and the ranked guards. He could see the prisons, deep below the sands.

God spoke for the last time and drove the smoke of fear from Moses's mind, and he looked and saw the Holy Mountain and knew that by coming to this place and speaking with God he had been changed. God had given him power not only over the people, but over man and beast, stick and stone. He gazed at the flesh of his hand and knew that he had only to will it to become leprous and it would be so. He willed and it was so. He willed again and his hand was clean flesh. He looked at his staff—a shepherd's tool, like this beside me here—and willed and it became a snake, a many-coloured serpent wriggling among the rocks. He willed again and his staff lay stiff at his feet. Then he understood that nothing in the world, not the scorn of the people nor the anger of Pharaoh, could make him afraid again. The only thing to fear was the God of the Holy Mountain.

He watched the flames die out of the tree, leaving it as green as before. He gathered his flock and drove them back to the camp of Jethro his father-in-law, and all the way he found water and pasture, even where none had been before. He took his leave of Jethro and travelled back into Egypt and there, as is well known, he smote the nation with plagues until Pharaoh himself was afraid, and let the people go.

THE PLAGUES OF EGYPT

Work-song, sung by a dozen or more women weaving a large hanging for Solomon's Temple. As they knot and shear their own sections of the traditional pattern, one chants the verse and the rest join the chorus. They sing each verse several times before moving on to the next. 950 BC.

Aaron took his staff and pointed at the river and the water turned to blood
Aaron took his staff and pointed at the river and the water turned to blood
 Every stream in Egypt, well and pond and puddle
 Jar and dish and bucket full of reeking scarlet
 Till Egypt howled for pity.

Chorus: So Pharaoh gave his promise and Moses spoke the word
And the streams ran clear, but did Pharaoh keep his promise? No!

Aaron took his staff and pointed at the marshes and the frogs came croaking out
 Horrible and slimy they gathered in the pathways
 They hopped about the courtyards, they piled up in the kitchens
 Till Egypt howled for pity.

Chorus: So Pharaoh gave his promise and Moses spoke the word
And the frogs went home, but did Pharaoh keep his promise? No!

Aaron took his staff and pointed at the desert and the lice came crawling in
 Moving like a river they fastened on the people
 They smothered sheep and cattle, they sucked the blood of Pharaoh
 Till Egypt howled for pity.

Chorus: So Pharaoh gave his promise and Moses spoke the word
And the lice all died, but did Pharaoh keep his promise? No!

Aaron took his staff and pointed at the cities and the flies came whining up
    Thicker than a sandstorm they settled on the middens,
    They settled on the foodstuffs, they buzzed around the palace
    Till Egypt howled for pity.

Chorus: Then Pharaoh gave his promise and Moses spoke the word
And the flies flew south, but did Pharaoh keep his promise? No!

Aaron took his staff and pointed at the meadows and the cattle-plague began
    Sores and boils and flakings, funguses and droolings
    Nests of maggots writhing on swine and sheep and oxen
    Till Egypt howled for pity.

Chorus: Then Pharaoh gave his promise and Moses spoke the word
And the sores all healed, but did Pharaoh keep his promise? No!

Aaron took his staff and pointed at the people and their skin broke out in boils
    The babies in their cradles, the princes in their mansions,
    The wizards in their wisdom all so horrible to look at
    That Egypt howled for pity.

Chorus: Then Pharaoh gave his promise and Moses spoke the word
And their skin was silk, but did Pharaoh keep his promise? No!

Aaron took his staff and pointed at the heavens and the hail came crashing down
    A million icy pebbles to flatten crop and vineyard
    To batter man and cattle, to shatter hut and palace
    Till Egypt howled for pity.

Chorus: Then Pharaoh gave his promise and Moses spoke the word
And the skies were clear, but did Pharaoh keep his promise? No!

Aaron took his staff and pointed to the desert and locusts bred and came
    A cloud to blot the sky out they settled upon Egypt
    They gobbled every orchard, every blade of every pasture
    Till Egypt howled for pity.

Chorus: Then Pharaoh gave his promise and Moses spoke the word
And the locusts fled, but did Pharaoh keep his promise? No!

Aaron took his staff and pointed at the sunrise and the Night-by-day began
 Darkness, thick as water, lay and brooded over Egypt
 Couldn't see to find your doorway, couldn't see to touch your children
 Till Egypt howled for pity.

Chorus: Then Pharaoh gave his promise and Moses spoke the word
And the sun shone strong, but did Pharaoh keep his promise? No!

Aaron took his staff, yes, he took his staff and broke it

Chorus: Ai! He broke his staff!

Aaron took his staff, yes he took his staff and broke it

Chorus: Ai! He broke his staff!

 God's dark and secret angel moved at midnight through all Egypt
 And Pharaoh's eldest son lay dead beneath his wing-tip
 And every eldest son in all the land of Egypt
 Then Egypt wailed in mourning.

Chorus: Then Pharaoh kept his promise for he understood the word
And we took our leave and we walked away from Egypt.
So!

THE TWELFTH PLAGUE

Told by a father hiding with his family in a cellar in Lydda, during the persecution of Antiochus Epiphanes. 168 BC.

———◆———

Sshhh . . . Wait . . . They've gone . . . You can bring the lamp out. Oh yes, they were the madman's soldiers. You learn to know the pace, heavy and slow, as if they were treading the pavement back into place . . .

Out? No, my darling, I'm afraid not. In any case your cousin Judas is in the gymnasium, wrestling naked with other boys, learning to be a good little Greek and not a Jew at all. If you go out the madman's soldiers will catch you and take you there too. And they will hurt you, my darling, to make you tell them why you have not been there before. And then they will come and find us and take us away, your mother and me . . . no, not to the gymnasium, to another place. And perhaps you will never see us again.

But it will end. Soon, my darling, soon, you will be able to play in the sun, and I shall open a little shop, much better than the one they burnt, and your mother will cook good food in a fine new kitchen. It will end, because that is the promise. Sit quiet and I will tell you a story. It is an old story, but because of what has happened I have been thinking about it in a new way.

Tell me now, what is different about the day after tomorrow? . . .

And what is the Passover? . . .

Yes, the night when the Angel of God passed over the houses of the Jews in Egypt and did them no harm, but killed the eldest child in every house of the Egyptians, so that Pharaoh would let the Jews leave.

Yes, I know that was what you meant. I only wanted to put it very plainly, because I am telling myself this story, just as much as I am telling it to you.

Why, my darling, why? No, I mean, why *that* event, of all the strange and marvellous works of God? Why should *that* be our chief feast, passed on from generation to generation?

In times of peace and plenty it did not seem strange, but it was. Last year, remember, we swept every room and polished everything that would shine and searched the house for yeast and your mother prepared a great feast—but before we ate we put on the table strange bits of food, burnt bone and biscuit and parsley and vinegar, and we held the ceremony, at the heart of which you asked the questions you had so carefully learnt and I answered by telling you the story of the Passover.

This year there will be no brass to polish, no feast to gobble at the end, but still we will hold the ceremony. It will seem strange, but it will not be so. For *this*, my darling, is why. It was for *this* that generation after generation the youngest child asked the questions and the fathers answered—that in the time of our darkness we should remember!

Listen, there was another madman in Egypt. They called him Pharaoh. He too wanted to make the Jews what they were not. The madman we call Antiochus wants to make us Greeks, for the increase of his glory. The madman they called Pharaoh wanted to make us Egyptian slaves, for the same reason.

Imagine the Egyptians, though—not Pharaoh and his officers, but the ordinary people under the lash of their merciless rulers—shopkeepers, farmers, masons, smiths. Even in good times they have troubles enough, but when bad times come, plague after plague, how can they bear it? A scapegoat must be found, someone to blame, to punish. You know we are the chosen people, my darling? Do you think it was only God who chose us? No, our enemies chose us too. Think of the rumours running unchecked: it is the Jews who have angered the river god so that he turns his water to blood; it is the Jews who infect the children with boils; the Jews whose witchcraft brings the flies out of the desert; the Jews, the Jews, the Jews!

Think of the mutters swelling to a growl, and the growl to a roaring. Think of the mob boiling out into the streets to smash and burn and loot. We have seen this, have we not, you and your mother and I?

The answer must have seemed so easy in Egypt, for the Jews were willing to go. Why not let them? Well, the rulers needed the Jews. They said they needed them to build their cities, but really they needed them so that their own subjects should have a dog to kick, a neighbour to despise, a victim to prevent them from realising that they themselves were victims . . .

But remember also the madman. He needs the Jews for his glory, for his power. They cannot choose to leave him, for that would be to allow them a choice which is not his choice, and so diminish that glory and that power.

But look, the Jews have found a leader, an educated man, one of Pharaoh's own household. What is more he is able to foretell the comings and goings of these plagues. Surely even a madman will listen to him . . .

Oh no . . . That would be to accept that the madman was wrong. The madman must be right! How, he asks, could the Jews know the cattle blight was coming unless they brought the disease? And did their own cattle suffer? No, and that proves that all the time the Jews had a secret cure . . .

You see? I think that perhaps in all rulers and all governments there are the seeds of this madness. In their own eyes they are the persecuted ones. They believe that they have powerful and secret enemies, who have knowledge which the rulers have a right to wring from them . . . hence in the end the madman's soldiers hunting us through the streets of our own city. Hence his prisons and his torturers.

Let us not think of that. Think instead of the other madman, blinded by his dream of glory so that no lesson can show him that the dream is untrue. A plague, a drought, a famine—*It is the Jews!* Then drive them out. *But they are my subjects. If they go my glory will be less.* The plague deepens, the springs stink. *Well let them go. My nature is generous.* Now the land is healed, the people feed fat. *Hold fast to the Jews! If I let them go because they threatened me, that would be weakness, and I must show that I am stronger even than this God of theirs.*

Time and again, my darling, time and again. But the repetition is not mere repetition—it is like the heartbeat in a nightmare, steady as a marching tread, but coming nearer, nearer . . .

And think of the Jews in Egypt, those loose tribes who had trekked there to escape a famine, had settled but remained strangers, and so become outcasts and slaves. No doubt at first when Moses called them they did not want to go. They did what we have always done in such times, shrugged their shoulders, slunk closer to the wall, taught their children not to be noticed. But slowly the tensions tautened until to survive for one day more was no longer any comfort. A new word spread along the alleyways: *Yes, we must go.*

A whisper only, like a voice in a dream. But the whisper becomes a real voice, Moses crying the word aloud among the tangled alleys, and those loose tribes which had so far merely jostled each other at random in the fight to survive, strain now all together in one direction, away from Egypt, towards that faintly remembered promise, the gift of a land in which they would not

be slaves. Remember this, my darling. Without the riots on the streets, without the madman on his throne, those tribes would never have become a nation, ready to obey one leader, eager to march when he gave the sign.

And what a sign! A rabbi has told me that long before the Passover there had been a festival at that season to celebrate the return of the spring and thank God for His gifts. So they kept it still in the crowded hovels of the cities, in the slave-quarters of the brutal farms, in the secret warrens where the hunted hid. That night word went out that not one family must forget the ritual, that in each household somehow the yeastless bread must be baked, the lamb of sacrifice roasted and its blood streaked on the doorpost. That night we were to be one nation, acting all together, praising God for His gifts, praising Him from the deeps of the pit, all with one voice.

It is written: "At midnight the Lord smote the first-born of the land of Egypt, from the first-born of Pharaoh who sat on the throne to the first-born of the captive in the dungeon. And there was a great cry in Egypt."

Think. Suppose God sent such a sign to the madman we call Antiochus, what would he do? *There must be an end*, he would say. *The Jews must go.* That, at least, is what Pharaoh said. But then it is written that he changed his mind yet again and sent an army of chariots to bring the Jews back. Can that be all his reason? It was the reason of madness, remember. Think of the footstep in the nightmare coming nearer, the last threads of logic snapping. *The Jews must go. But not to any place. There must be an end. But how? Not here, in cities, where my slave-people can see. Out in the desert, then. The sands will cover their bones.*

Think then of this new nation marching in fear and wonder towards their remembered promise. Think of the soldiers riding behind, just out of sight over the horizon, waiting for a place where the Jews can be trapped, unable to scatter. So they come at last to the place which is no place, a long slope of dunes running down to a flat and reedy sea, and no road further. Here is the finish which the madman has planned. There will be empty desert, and the vultures gathering, and the soldiers riding home with no captives.

But God works in His own way. He includes even the minds of madmen in His pattern of love. He made a road through the sea where no road was. He brought Israel out of Egypt with a strong hand.

So *this* is why, my darling. Generation after generation, through the easy times of peace, your ancestors have taught their children the ritual so that now, in the time of our darkness, we shall be able to join, one loved and loving family, and as we say the ancient words know that God's promise has not staled or tarnished, and that He will find for us, too, a road . . .

Shh . . . Listen . . . Hide the lamp—another patrol! Still now!

THE RED SEA

Told by a peasant fisherman on the Red Sea shore to an Egyptian official
making a tour of inspection. A hundred years after the Exodus—about
1200 BC.

The monument, Lord? You cannot read the symbols? Lord, Lord, it is not my fault! Do not whip me! They built it of the softest stone they could find, and they gave my father's grandfather a papyrus which I cannot read, but which my father showed your honour's predecessor and *he* gave my father silver for faithfulness to duty. The papyrus is in my hut, Lord, but I know its teaching, for my father made me learn it word by word. It says that my family must guard the monument and on pain of death let no man touch it, even to restore the symbols.

My Lord will trust my word? I kiss the ground my Lord has trod on!

The story? Lord, I do not know. It is just the monument of Pharaoh's victory. We fishermen use it as a sea-mark . . . Do not whip me, Lord! . . . Arrh!

My Lord is merciful! His whip is like the sun, which scorches the earth— but how should man live without it? Let me rest a little, and then I will tell my Lord what my father told me . . .

It is secret knowledge. The great soldier-lord who caused the monument to be built gave my father's grandfather orders to forget all that he had seen— but how should he forget such a thing? Shall the sun forget to rise? Shall my Lord forget to be glorious?

My father's grandfather was a young man, not yet married, when he saw

73

these things. First came strangers. There was no rumour of their coming. They spoke our language when they wished, but among themselves they spoke otherwise. They came out of the west, by night. The dunes had been empty at nightfall, but beyond the topmost ridge my father's grandfather had seen a wonder. In the sunset it seemed to be a sandstorm, gathered into a dark and whirling pillar such as we sometimes see along these shores, though not at that season. He watched it to see whether it was coming this way, because then there would be a need to lash the boat down and heap boulders on the roof against the whirlwind; but as the sky darkened the pillar changed its nature and glowed with a light as though the sun were trapped within it. So it remained, long after all the stars were bright. Then he became afraid and hid within the hut and prayed to all the gods whose names he could remember. At midnight there was a murmuring of voices, but still he hid. When he looked out in the morning the dunes were full of people.

After a while he lost his fear and went among them. They were a strange people. They drove cattle, and sheep, and goats, flock upon flock, though there is scarcely grazing for twenty sheep between here and Bitter Springs. They had journeyed all night and were too weary to march further. Besides, where was there to go? They told my father's grandfather that a great wizard had led them to this point, promising them a land of rich grazing, and now all they saw was the salt sea. They were very bitter against this wizard, but afraid of him also. Indeed, all the while they stayed on the dunes the black whirlwind hovered just beyond the second reed-bed my Lord can see up the shore there. The demon this wizard worshipped was inside the whirlwind. It made no noise and caused no breeze along the shore.

So they rested, a great horde, like locusts. They watered their animals from the good spring behind the hut. We own the water-rights, but they paid no money though they took all the water there was.

At noon some of their chieftains came to the hut and asked my father's grandfather whether there was any way of crossing through the sea. Now, Lord, at certain seasons, when the tide and the wind work together, the water goes down and sand spits appear, so that a man can walk and wade almost from one shore to the other, though there are still two channels where he must swim. But at the season when the strangers came these spits were covered by more than the depth of a man. This my father's grandfather told them, and they went away discontented.

He did not go fishing that day, knowing that the strangers would steal his nets and pots if he left them unguarded. In the middle of the afternoon he was down by the shore, mending nets, when a great cry went up along the

dunes and looking up he saw what the strangers had seen. Along the ridge there, bright as the sun, shone the armour of soldiers and of chariots—just such as accompany my Lord to proclaim his glory, but hundreds upon hundreds of them. From the strangers' shouting he saw that they thought the soldiers were their enemies, though they were the servants of great Pharaoh and protectors of all loyal men. The strangers gathered around the great boulder my Lord can see up there. A man climbed onto the boulder and stood above them. The strangers shouted at him, cursing him in their own language with voices full of fear and weeping. He raised his arms and they were silent. He spoke to them for a little while, then turned and spoke in a different voice to the whirlwind, so my father's grandfather knew him to be the wizard.

He had power, Lord, for at the sound of his voice the whirlwind moved. All watched in silence and fear as it slid up the dunes, spreading wider and wider as it travelled, until it stretched in a roaring cloud all along the slopes below the ridge, throwing the sand this way and that, full of lightnings and loud hissings. We know sandstorms well along this coast and are not afraid of them. You stay in your hut if you can, but if you must go out you wrap your face round well and provided you know the lie of the land you will be all right. This was no such storm. The gods themselves would have feared to pass through it. The soldiers stayed beyond the ridge and were not seen again that day.

At evening the wizard went down to the shore and stood between the second and third reed-beds, where the first sandspit begins. The strangers gathered round him in silence and watched while he raised his arms and stretched them towards the further shore, calling in a strong voice.

My Lord sees how still the water lies today. So it was then. But at the calling of the wizard the water over by the far shore began to darken with the shadow which we fishermen call Demon-breath. It is the mark a squall makes as it roughens the surface. Even on a still day you can see it moving along, like cloud-shadow. So my father's grandfather saw it move, answering the wizard's calling, wriggling along the water like a great serpent. The noise of its coming grew almost as loud as the storm along the hills. The water frothed, and humped back from the path of the squall. Spume blew up off the sea, drenching the strangers where they stood, but they held their ground and waited, leaning against the wind with their cloaks pressed hard against their bodies and swirling out behind. All the while my father's grandfather watched from the point where the monument is now, without a breath of wind stirring his beard. By nightfall he could see the top of the first sandspit beginning to show, though it was then high tide.

When he woke in the morning the strangers were gone. He went back to the point and saw that the wind still blew from the east, but the whirlwind had gathered itself closer together and was quieter now, hovering along the shore by the reed-beds. All the way between shore and shore the sand-spits showed clear, dry as the dunes. The water still frothed on either side, held back by the wizard-summoned wind. Half-way across he could see the last of the strangers, driving their flocks along this pathway. He could not tell whether the first of them had reached the other shore—look, my Lord, it is too far to see.

The soldiers of Pharaoh had come down from the hills and were drawn up along the dunes. The cloud concealed the pathway from them. When my father's grandfather saw them he hid, which was well. There is a gully that cuts in close under the point where a man may stand and look out to sea but not be seen from above. Soon after he had hidden he heard voices on the point above him. They spoke court-language, of which he could understand one word in three, but from their tones he guessed that it was the lord who commanded the soldiers, come to the point with some of his officers so that he could see what was happening beyond the cloud. This lord was angry. He blamed his wizard for not making a magic as strong as the magic of the strangers. The officers who answered him were frightened, and not only of his anger. Suddenly they began to call out, and looking towards the sea my father's grandfather saw that the cloud had gathered itself into a pillar as before and was moving along the pathway between the waters, faster than a man could run. The funnel of wind still blew fiercely from the east but the cloud moved against it as though it were made of some stuff which the wind could not touch.

The lord shouted orders. Some of the officers started to protest but there was a clatter of metal and a groan. Then trumpets sounded along the shore and the chariots started to drive out over the pathway, the horses trying to rear and shy away from the wind and the banked and frothing waves on either side, and their drivers lashing them on. They drove fast, as though the sand were smooth rock. The chariots bounced. A man fell, but the horses behind raced over him and he did not rise.

When all the chariots were on the pathway, the last as far as a shout might carry on a still day, the wind from the east blew suddenly more strongly, whipping the sand off the spits this way and that. The cloud swept back over the soldiers and vanished. When it had gone my father's grandfather saw that the surface of the pathway had changed and become soft, like the dunes. The chariots sank in the softness up to their axles. The horses heaved and floundered. Some of the chariots turned and began to come back, very slowly, moving like things in a dream.

Then the wind died and the waters on either side of the pathway closed like the lips of a mouth, and all the soldiers were gone.

My father's grandfather, very frightened, stayed in his hiding-place. Again he heard the voice of the soldier-lord, speaking in the language my Lord uses to me, so he knew the lord was speaking to common soldiers.

"You three men of my guard," he said. "I make you captains of troops. Witness this: in the name of Great Pharaoh I declare war on the sea. Any man who returns from the water has fled from the face of the enemy and must be executed on the spot for cowardice. Go down to the brink now and kill any who come ashore."

The men moved off. The soldier-lord spoke again, in court-language. My father's grandfather understood the word for "wizard", and later when another voice replied he understood talk about poison in cooking-pots. He saw the three guards pacing the shore. Some horses came out, two with soldiers clinging to them. These the guards killed with swords and threw them back in the water. At last he heard the soldier-lord shout to the guards that they need watch the shore no longer and that food was prepared for them. He hid all afternoon and came out, very weary, in the dusk. There were four fresh graves in the sand by the hut and the tracks of a single chariot going away over the hill.

The monument, Lord? Yes, many days after workmen came. They dragged a great stone on a sledge. My father's grandfather spoke to one of the overseers, asking why they did not bring stone from the quarry down at Redcliff. It is good hard stone there, and they could have floated it up the water at one-tenth of the cost. The overseer told him that the orders specified soft sandstone for the monument. He read the symbols aloud. It told of Pharaoh's great victory over the sea. The overseer gave my father's grandfather the papyrus of which I told my Lord. When my father's grandfather asked him the reason for all these things the overseer cursed him for a fool, and said that Great Pharaoh's armies are always victorious but there are certain victories which are best forgotten.

My Lord, how can we forget? Still when we fish our nets bring up the bones of horses, or bridles, or parts of a chariot-wheel . . . What does my Lord mean? Have mercy, my Lord, have mercy! I have no son, no one to tell the story to! When I die it *will* be forgotten! Have mercy . . .

THE SONG OF MIRIAM

*Told and sung by a mother who is rehearsing her daughter for the
annual Dance of the Women that celebrated the Red Sea crossing. During
the wanderings in the desert, about 1300 BC.*

———◆———

Good. So you follow your cousin Rachel as we snake among the tents, using
that step all the time. As your left foot goes forward you make the tambourine
clash. That's right . . . Again . . . Again . . . Five clashes and then the
words. I'll sing them with you . . . Now!

> Sing to God
> For He has triumphed in glory!
> Horse and charioteer
> He has hurled into the sea!

SINAI

Told by an old man sitting by his doorway while his grand-daughters
bring out food ready for returning harvesters—they scarcely hear him.
Soon after the conquest of Canaan, about 1200 BC.

Milk and honey! A land flowing with milk and honey! What good is that, when the men have all become as soft as women, soft as little girls? Where are the real men now, the men who wiped out the Amorites? The men who burnt Ai, who broke the walls of Jericho as though they'd blown them down with their breath? All dead. Where are the men who knew the desert? Dead, all dead.

I tell you, God forged us in the desert. Like a smith hammering bronze He hammered Israel. He made the people His sword, and the desert was His anvil.

Oh, we were soft stuff when we came out of Egypt. Slaves. I was not born, but from my own father's mouth I have heard the story, a boy born in slavery, reared to be a slave. But was he a slave when I knew him? No! Yet they whined like slaves all the way to Sinai—"Why did you bring us here? We had water and bread in Egypt, and roofs to sleep under. Here there's nothing but starvation and thirst and the desert sky. Let's go back. We'd rather be slaves than dead."

That's what they said. To Moses himself, to his own face!

Yes, I have seen Moses. I have stood at the door of the tent of the man who talked with God! Who else can say the same? No one, I tell you. They're all dead.

Let me tell you what happened at Sinai. Stop that clattering around with pots for these soft farmers and listen to the voice of one who was born at the foot of that mountain, while it smoked with the presence of God!

No, first look. Out there, where the sky is yellowest, there lies Egypt—not so far away, less than a month's march. Yet we were forty years in the desert. Why didn't Moses bring the people straight to this land, which God had promised them? Because they were soft. They would have had to fight their way all up the coastal strip, and at the first skirmish they would have scampered back to Egypt like the slaves they were. That's why God told Moses to lead them south, down into the empty places, where He could forge his people, make them men. At Sinai the hammer struck the anvil, and the work began.

They camped below the mountain. It seemed a place like any other place in the desert—nothing to eat and nothing to drink and sand that stung in the wind like a whip and bare rock that seared you if you touched it and this one great hummocky hill. They camped there because Moses had found a stream. He could always find water—we used to say he had only to strike his staff into the ground and a spring would spout up. So the people rested by the stream. God sent flocks of little birds, flying low and weary, and they caught them with nets spread between bushes. It was a good place for manna, too. Yes, I have eaten manna—you find it in certain hollows in the desert, a little round stuff, like seeds, greyish white and soft. You have to eat it the day you gather it or it rots. It isn't milk and honey, no! It tastes of nothing much, but those who eat it become men!

After several days a storm began to gather on the mountain-top, a great dark cloud that seemed to promise rain. They were happy for that. It doesn't often rain in the desert, but when it does it is like a juggler's trick. The water streams down, and dry gullies become yellow roaring torrents and then the rain is gone. But next morning all the brown bare places are green with soft growth for the animals to eat—plants that have waited thirty years for this moment.

But no rain came. Only the cloud thickened and thickened on the mountain until it was like a piece of the blackest blackness of night hovering there in the glare of noon. There was no wind. Nothing moved at all. The animals forgot to graze and stood like rocks. The children stilled from their games. Babies woke but lay motionless in their wrappings, staring at the sky. All the people stood watching the cloud on the mountain-top, full of fear.

There were lightnings in the cloud, and thunder. The mountain began to shake. The thunder pieced itself together and became the sound of a ram's horn, but far louder than a man could blow, and longer than many men's breath could hold. It changed again and was a voice, the voice of God, speaking to the people. New-born, just five days old, I lay in my wrappings and heard the thunder speak the Ten Great Words. Yes, those Words which every child of Israel knows, which are the very heart of the Law, these ears first heard them spoken by the voice of God. Who else can say the same? They are all dead.

On Sinai all the people heard them, but they understood them no more than I did, a child new-born. Such a child knows the sound of its mother's voice but not what she is saying. So the people knew it was the voice of God, but could not know His meaning. When the voice stopped and became thunderings once more they were loosed from the trance that had held them. For a while they staggered about, almost mad with fear. Some ran into their tents and hid. Some lay down where they were and covered their heads with their coats. But many ran looking for Moses, to ask what the voice meant, and what they should do. They found him at the edge of the camp, gazing quietly towards the cloud that lay all along the ridge of the mountain.

They gathered round him, too afraid to whine or clamour. Somebody was pushed forward to speak for them. He fell on his knees before Moses.

"Don't let it happen again," he said, "or we will all go mad. Speak to this cloud, this God. If it has Words for us, ask it to tell them to you, alone, and then you can give us its orders. We will obey. The people will obey!"

Moses said nothing. He did not seem to see the man or hear him, but with his eyes still set on the cloud, he began to walk towards the ridge. Easily, as though he was following a broad smooth path through the scrub-trees and the tumbled boulders, he glided up the slope. The whisper spread among the tents and even those who had hidden came out to watch him until he vanished into the cloud. They waited. Lightning glimmered still among the darkness, but the thunder quietened and when it sounded it seemed to be the voice again, far off.

"It is speaking to Moses, alone," the people said. "It is not angry."

They went back to their tents.

Night came, and passed, and a day, and another day. Nothing new happened. The cloud smoked on the mountain and its lightnings came and went, but they were used to it, and when they heard the voice they thought, "Perhaps it is only thunder." But when on the third evening Moses had not come back they began to be afraid in a new way.

"It has eaten him," some of them said. "He has made himself the sacrifice for us."

Others said that the cloud would not give Moses back until the people made an offering. Many others were simply tired with the desert and wanted some new happening, and others still were afraid of the cloud and wanted something else to fill their minds . . . My father would never tell me how it came about, but he told me this. Listen.

It was night. They had built a fire and an altar, and on the altar they had set up an image, the image of a bull. It was hung with rich cloths and jewels they had brought out of Egypt. The altar dripped with the blood of sacrifices, so that the jewels and the blood glistened in the firelight. The drums rattled and the horns bellowed, and some of the men stripped naked and smeared themselves with the blood of sacrifices and leaped around the bull and slashed at their own limbs with knives, while the rest of the people watched, and beat their hands in rhythm with the drums, and shouted aloud with the dancers.

In the middle of the music and shouting, silence fell. There was no signal, no thunderclap, but the noise stopped all together in an instant, my father said, as though he had gone deaf. The dancers stood still. Everybody turned and saw Moses coming down from the mountain. They could see him far off, for all it was pitch night, because his face and all his flesh gleamed bright as the moon. Stiff in their places they watched in terror as he came down among them. He said no word but he walked up to the image of the bull, which it had taken six men to lift into its place on the altar, and he heaved it up and tossed it into the fire, where the flames wrapped round it, clay and cloth and jewels, and burnt it as though it had been straw.

Still without a word spoken men who a moment before had been shouting and clapping with the rest came out from among the crowd and cut down the dancers where they stood. They moved among the tribes, killing here and there, seeming to know without being told who was chosen to die. The people was born in blood, I tell you.

For a long while nobody stirred, then a wind came down from the mountain and passed across the place where they sat, and as it touched them those who still lived went quietly to their tents.

But Moses stood all night at the spot where the image of the bull had stood, looking towards the mountain, his face gleaming like the moon. And when they woke in the morning the cloud had vanished from the ridge.

But look at them down there now! Seed-sowers! Earth-scrabblers! Was it for them the mountain smoked? Was it for this God thundered, and the people was born in blood? Just that we should finish here, soft as Egyptian slaves, babbling about milk and honey?

FOUR
THE GIVEN LAND

 HE PERIOD OF THE JUDGES—ABOUT 1300–1020 BC. Moses dies. Under the leadership of Joshua the tribes—descended from the sons of Jacob—cross Jordan from the east. They destroy Jericho and drive out the weaker hill-tribes. A long struggle begins for the control of the fertile plains. At last the main enemy is the Philistines, a sea people (perhaps from Crete) who have settled in a confederation of city-states along the coast. In these wars a series of Judges lead the tribal armies.

GIBEON

Told by a slave on one of the farms which support the great shrine at Gilgal. Period of the Judges, about 1150 BC.

———◆———

Worse things happen than having to eat stale bread. It's a life, after all—food and a roof over your head. Would you rather be dead, a thin ghost whining in Sheol? Well, I'd rather be a slave and breathe real air into real lungs, and feel my stomach fat with real bread, stale but real.

No choice? I suppose not—not nowadays. We had the choice once, though, and to my mind we chose right. We're survivors, we Gibeonites. You don't meet many Jericho folk these days, or people out of Ai, do you? And why not? Because they chose the other way, that's why, and they're dead. All gone. Gibeon's a fine town still, isn't it, while there's not a stone standing in Jericho or Ai?

Remember when we pulled the old barn down by the ford, what sport we had killing the rats? It was like that when They came, only the people of Canaan were the rats, and it was Them that did the hunting. They came over Jordan, out of the East, and the first bit of civilisation they ran into was Jericho, with Jericho folk grinning at them from the tops of the walls. What could a lot of wild men out of the desert do against walls like that? The only thing Jericho folk didn't know was that They had It with them. Some sort of god—yes, what They worship up at Twelve Stones now—not a proper god with hoofs and horns, but . . . well, I've never heard of any god with hoofs and horns who could have done to Jericho what They and It did. By the time

86

They'd finished, those walls were flat and there wasn't a cockroach, hardly, moving anywhere in the ruins. They'd gone through the city killing everything that breathed—man, woman and child, mules, cattle, dogs, chickens, everything—as a sacrifice to It.

Same at Ai. They set an ambush outside the town with half their force and attacked with the other half. All together They weren't as many as there were fighting men in Ai, so when only half of Them came whooping up at the gates the men of Ai rushed out and counter-attacked. The half who'd been attacking ran off with the men of Ai charging after, but then that first half stood ground and the half who'd been in ambush closed in between the men of Ai and the city. You'd have thought the men of Ai could have fought their way back, easy. Only It turned their blood to water and they stood where they were and waited to be cut down. Then They went into Ai and treated it like Jericho. They hanged the King of Ai on a tree.

No more Jericho, no more Ai, but Gibeon's still there, isn't it? We're survivors, I tell you. We worked out, soon as we saw it wasn't any use standing up against Them and It, we'd better have a treaty. In my grandfather's time this was.

Only trouble, They weren't making any treaties. It had told Them It wanted everybody wiped out between Jordan and the sea. So how do you make a treaty with a people who'll slice you up as soon as you tell them you live here? You make them think otherwise, that's how.

First we chose our deputation, a scrawny lot of men with limps and bad backs and so on. Then we rounded up all the oldest mules we could find and hunted through the town for a lot of rotten old sacks and wine-skins. We cut holes in the deputation's clothes and half-tore their sandals, and we filled their sacks with mouldy bread and their skins with sour wine, and as they trooped out of the town gate the women stood on the tower and poured baskets of dust on them.

Deputation only had to get as far as Twelve Stones, where They were camped, less than three days' march from Gibeon, but by the time they'd got there it looked as if they'd come from the end of the world. I'm not saying they weren't nervous, looking this way and that in case It might tell somebody where they really came from, but all went well. Sentries stopped them, and speaking as foreign as they could they made signs they wanted to see the Head Man. So they were let into the camp and went limping and hobbling to where the Head Man was sitting with his captains. They flung themselves onto the ground in front of him and grovelled.

"What do you want?" said the Head Man.

(Now, mind you, the deputation had to tell the truth all the time, because they guessed It was sure to jump on them as soon as they lied.)

"We are your servants," they cried. "We want your friendship. We have heard that you are mighty warriors and your God has done great wonders for you. You smashed Jericho—is that the name?—and another mighty city—is it called Ia?"

"Ai," said the Head Man. "Where do you come from, not to know the true names of these places?"

"Over there," they said, pointing. "Long journey. Long, long journey."

(I suppose three days' march is a longish way if you've sore feet and bad backs and your mules keep falling down.)

"How far?" said the Head Man.

They looked at each other. They'd drunk a good deal of the wine on the journey, to take their minds off their backs and their feet, not to say having to face up to It and Them.

"Lost count," they said. "Long, long journey."

The Head Man looked at their torn clothes and broken sandals and decrepit mules and patched sacks and skins and the dust that covered them all. The deputation became nervous.

"We bring food for the feast," said one of them. "Only perhaps not very good now."

And they tipped the mouldy bread out of the sacks and poured the sour wine into cups and offered them round, apologising and explaining that the bread had once been fresh-baked and the wine sweet as man could wish. The Head Man and the captains sipped a bit and nibbled a bit, and then, as much to get the taste out of their mouths as anything, they shouted for fresh food and offered it round among the deputation, so each lot ate the other's food.

While they were eating the Head Man says to one of the deputation, "What's the name of this city of yours?"

"Gibeon," said our man, wishing he were back home there.

"Gibeon!" cried the Head Man. "That's between Jordan and the sea. That's the next town we're attacking! What do you mean, telling me you came from the other end of the earth? Gibeon's only three days' march away!"

"It's a long way if you've sore feet," they said. "Do not be angry with us, mighty servant of It-who-has-no-name! There is nothing you can do. You have eaten our bread and we have eaten yours."

"You have tricked me," said the Head Man. "You cannot trick God."

"We told you the truth. It made no thunder. Everything we said was true. The bread was once fresh-baked, and the wine sweet."

The Head Man was just about to rage at them again when he stuck. He had one arm half raised and his head was cocked a little sideways as if he was listening to something. All the captains fell silent, and the deputation stared, for fifty heart-beats or more. Then the Head Man came unstuck with a long sigh. He smiled.

"Everything you have told me is the truth?" he asked in a gentle voice.

"Yes, yes," the deputation clamoured, sure of their triumph now.

"Very well," he said. "We will take it to be so and swear our treaty with you. But what were the first words you spoke?"

They looked at each other. They couldn't remember. They had been too nervous.

"Just some formal politeness," one of them muttered.

"The first words you spoke were 'We are your servants,'" he told them. "I take it that this is true also?"

You see? They had fallen into their own trap. If they tried to tell him it was just a form of words, he would be able to say that they had lied to him and the treaty was invalid and slice them up and do to Gibeon what he'd done to Jericho and Ai. There was nothing for it. They were his servants.

So the treaty was made, and I must say They have stuck by it. First thing that happened, five kings came down with their armies from the north to punish Gibeon for making a treaty with Them, but They came out from Gilgal, marching all night, and fell on the besiegers at dawn and slaughtered them and drove them off, and killed all five kings by the cave of Makkedah. They don't like having us living here among them, but They'll stick by the treaty for ever because they swore to in the presence of It.

And our side is we provide them with slaves for the shrines, and the shrine-farms. Bad luck it's you and me, but look at it this way. Wouldn't you rather your grandfather was a Gibeonite than that he'd been born in Jericho or Ai? Then you wouldn't have been here at all, would you?

JUDGE OVER ISRAEL

Told by an old shepherd to a younger one as they sort fleeces to pay the
tax-gatherer. Manasseh territory, time of Solomon, 920 BC.

. . . seventeen for us, then one for the King, two for the King and three for
the King. Start again. One for us . . . Hey! That last one for the King, that's no
good, that's all warbled. Swap it with one of ours.

Do what I say, boy. Don't you remember what happened two summers
back, when Beriah tried to get away with sending the King warbled fleeces?
Better safe than sorry, *I* say. No point in grumbling, either. Taxes are here to
stay. Now we've got Kings we're bound to have taxes.

Always had Kings? That's what comes of not having a father. No one to tell
a boy what he ought to know. Of course we didn't always have Kings, and
then there weren't taxes, only shrine-dues, which weren't so bad. Where was
I? Two for us . . . three for us . . .

Well, not unless you count the Judges, but they weren't like Kings. We
didn't have Judges all the time, only when things were bad and we needed
them. What used to happen was first things were good, no raiders, no
famines, plenty of grazing, fat harvests, and the people would enjoy it all and
forget about God. Like as not they'd start worshipping Baal-trash, even. Then
God would let the foreigners come in plundering and taking over, to remind
us we couldn't get along without Him, and when we'd learnt the lesson he'd
send us a Judge to raise the tribes and drive the foreigners out. Happened
time after time. Some people never learn. Four for us . . . five . . .

Oh, from any of the tribes that needed one. Must have depended on who was suffering from foreigners at the time. Deborah, she was from Ephraim for instance, and Jephthah—the one who had bad luck with his daughter—was from Gilead. I've even heard a fellow from Dan claiming *they* had a Judge called Samson, but he didn't sound the right sort from what he said about him. We had a Judge of our own, too, right here in Manasseh.

Gideon, that's right . . .

No, no, no—you've got it all mixed up. Look, Gideon began as a man like you or me except that he must have had a bit of ploughland of his own, because he had a harvest to thresh. That's where it starts. Gideon was thresh-ing his harvest, and what's more he was doing it in a wine-press, spite of the dust, because he didn't want the Midianites to see what he was up to. There'd been hordes of them, raiding in over the hills on their camels, just around harvest time when all the work had been done and they could simply snatch the crops and go. Gideon would be expecting another raid, and be trying to get his harvest in early, and in secret.

All at once there was a stranger standing by him. What's more the stranger knew Gideon's name, though he never gave his own. He started in with no greetings at all.

"Gideon," says he, "hear the word of the Lord. The Midianites are sent to plague Israel for praying to the Baals. Now you must break down the Baal altars, and after that get an army together and drive out the Midianites."

Yes, a tall order all right. I don't know what Gideon said, but at least he had to offer the stranger food. When he brought it out the stranger told him to put it on a rock. He did so, and then the stranger touched the food with the tip of his staff and fire came out of the rock and burnt the food away. As soon as that was done, he vanished.

Take care what you say, my lad! Been there to see it, indeed! When God makes something Holy happen, He doesn't do it just for people to stare at! Holy means dangerous! Anyway, Gideon understood that the sign was for him, so he dropped his flail, left the harvest half-threshed, took an axe out of his shed and marched down to the nearest Baal altar. He smashed it up and chopped down their filthy pillar. A crowd gathered, so he picked men from them to take the horns and sound them all through the hills, calling the tribes to war—Manasseh of course, but Zebulun too, and Asher, and Naphthali. While that was happening he sent out scouts to look for the raiders, and they found a whole horde of them, half Midianites and half Amalekites, camped in a valley up by Mount Gilboa.

Now remember, these were raiders, jumpy as a cat. There was no hope of catching them by just marching up with a horde of untrained tribesmen—they'd have gone before he got there. So first Gideon told anybody to go home that didn't feel like fighting. Unvolunteered them, if you see what I mean. That still left him with far more men than he could use, so he set them a series of tests, watched the way they drank at a brook, for instance—whether they kept their eyes open or whether they simply got down on their knees and lapped. That way he picked the ones who knew about desert raiding. Whittled his army down to three hundred, they say.

He told each man to find a jar and a lamp and a ram's-horn trumpet and bring them along, and then he set out to catch the enemy, moving at night, hiding by day. He could never have done that with the great rabble that volunteered in the first place, you see.

Early on the second night he came up with them, still in the valley where they'd been found. His men lit their lamps but hid them in the pots. They split in three and crept round along the hills. In the dead middle of the night he blew a blast on his own horn, and all round the hills the men took up the sound. They took the lamps out of jars and they smashed the jars on the nearest rock and yelled like fiends. That valley was full of echoes, too.

Imagine you're one of the Midianites. Your saddlebags are full of booty and you're anxious to get home—in fact you've spent the last couple of days arguing with the Amalekites whether to stay or go, because they've not been so lucky as you have and want to carry on with the raid. There've been lost tempers and you're more than half afraid they might try taking your booty off you. Now, in the middle of the night, without any warning from the sentries or any rumour of enemies near by, you are woken by the sound of war-horns, and yells, and the smash and clatter of fighting. You jump up, snatch your sword, and see lights all round. A man blunders against you in the dark. "Who's there?" you cry. By his answer you know he's an Amalekite. You hack him down.

Once that's started, it doesn't stop. They were at each other's throats all night. All the tribesmen had to do was put their lamps on the ground, wait a few paces behind them, and cut down anyone who tried to make a break for it through the ring of light. Of course quite a few got out, but the rest of Gideon's army were waiting for them all along the hills, and not many came home. So thanks to Gideon there was no more trouble from the Midianites for a very long time.

After? Well, he was honoured in Manasseh, and that was only fair, but it seems to have gone to his head. He took a lot of wives and had a whole pack of sons, but there's none of his line left that I know of. When he died one of

his sons killed off almost all the others and set himself up as King of Shechem, but it did him no good. A woman dropped a millstone on his head while he was besieging Thebez, and that was the end of him. Funny how often you get that—a good man breeding bad. Lucky it doesn't happen the same with sheep.

How far'd we got? Five in that last pile? Six for us, then, seven . . .

SAMSON AND DELILAH

Sung by an old woman in the tribe of Dan, in the far north.
About 1000 BC.

Soft, soft her whisper all the night
   While in his arms she lay:
"What makes you stronger than the lion
   That leaps upon its prey?"

"Let you but seven bow-strings take,
   By arrow undefiled,
And bind them all about my limbs—
   I'm weak as any child."

She's bound him round with seven strings
   (O but his dreams were sweet).
In rush the foe. He's burst the bonds
   And slain them at her feet.

"O mock me not, you man of might,
   For you I love alone.
What makes you stronger than the horse
   That stamps upon the stone?"

"But weave my hair in seven knots
   And hold it with yon pin
That you upon your shoulder wear,
   And all my strength you'll win."

In seven knots she's woven his locks
   (O but his dreams were fair).
In rush the foe. The pin slides free.
   He's slain them on the stair.

"You mock and mock, you man of might,
   But love is still to prove.
What makes you stronger than the bear,
   Lurks in the mountain grove?"

"But take and shear one lock of the hair
   That curls about my head.
It never felt the blade before—
   And I would that I were dead."

Twixt night and morn she's ta'en and shorn
   (O but his dreams were ill).
In rush the foe. His strength is gone.
   They've bound him to their will.

They've rent away his brave brown eyes,
   His limbs they've chained withal.
They've carried him down before their King,
   Was feasting in the hall.

Before the King he makes them sport
   Who once had made them woe.
"Now let me rest against yon beam,
   For I am brought full low.

"O God of battles, look you down,
   Remember Israel's pain.
That I may lesson these Philistines
   Give me my strength again."

He's laid his arm about the beam,
   He's bowed his mighty back.
For this one hour he has his power.
   They hear the roof-tree crack.

O many and many a heathen lord
   Rode to the feast that day.
The little foxes came out at eve
   To carry their bones away.

O many and many a lady fair
   Died in the roof-tree's fall,
And Samson, Judge of Israel,
   Lay in the midst of all.

THE CALLING OF SAMUEL

Told by a priest instructing a new intake of boys to be trained in the
Temple service. Time of the later Kings, about 700 BC.

Now my young friends, this is your first morning as servants of the House of God. You are all sons of the house of Aaron, so your fathers have taught you what it means to become a priest, but you still have many things to learn, and there is much that will be strange to you. We will not start on that today. Instead I am going to tell you a story.

Who here knows the story of Samuel?

You all do? Excellent. And how did you learn it?

Your fathers told you—just as it should be. My own father told it to me, too, when I was your age—about a thousand and one years ago. Now I am going to tell it to you all over again, because from today you are all young Samuels, and it is important that you should all know the same story.

It begins at Shiloh. In those days the Ark of the Covenant rested in a shrine at Shiloh, because the great King David had not yet captured Jerusalem and made it God's Holy City. There was a chief priest at Shiloh, a good old man—like me. His name was Eli, and his sons were bad boys—like you. I think Eli forgot to beat the badness out of them, but don't worry—I shan't make the same mistake with you. And when those boys grew up Eli allowed them to become priests of God, at Shiloh, though now they were bad men. So God had two bad priests at Shiloh. Remember this—it is important in the story.

One morning Eli was at his place in the courtyard before the shrine when he saw a woman kneeling there, throwing herself about, whispering, muttering, weeping. He thought she was drunk—all Israel used to make pilgrimages to Shiloh in those days and feast and rejoice when they got there, so he wasn't surprised. But I told you he was a kind old man. He went and raised her gently from the ground.

"You oughtn't to come in here drunk," he said. "Go and get sober and come back and say your prayers then. God doesn't much care for drunkards."

She shook her head, still weeping, and tried to explain that she wasn't drunk, only unhappy. She had no children, and her husband's other wife had several and used to mock her for her barrenness, and she was afraid that her husband, though he was a good man, would soon stop loving her.

Eli had heard the same sort of story many, many times, but he was still able to be sorry for her. He let her kneel as before and he prayed beside her for a while that she should have a child, and sent her away a little happier.

A year later she was happier still, because God had heard their prayers and she had a son. She called him Samuel—who here knows what that means? Yes, *I have asked him of God*. And because God had granted her asking she decided to give the child back to God as soon as he was old enough. So when he was still a bit younger than you are, she and her husband made the pilgrimage to Shiloh, just as before, and they found Eli there, just as before, and the woman made Samuel stand before him.

"My lord," she said. "This is the boy who was born after you prayed with me that I should have children. Now I want to give him back to God, to serve God here at Shiloh as long as he lives."

I have often wondered whether Eli remembered anything about her. He must have seen a lot of pilgrims since then, heard a lot of barren women weeping and praying—you will hear them too. Still, he looked at the boy and saw that he was sturdy and had a straightforward gaze, and he remembered the greedy, sidelong glances of his own sons, and he thought *When I am gone, God will need one honest servant here at Shiloh*. So he agreed. He accepted the sacrifices the father had brought, and arranged that the woman should come and see Samuel every year and bring him a new priest's robe. So they went home, leaving Samuel behind. I'm glad to say the woman had three more sons and two daughters.

The years, and the pilgrimages, and the feasts all went by. Eli grew old and blind; his sons grew wickeder; and Samuel simply grew up. He was almost a man before we come to the next part of the story.

Where did I say the Ark was kept at Shiloh? That's right—in a shrine. Here we keep it in the Holy of Holies, behind the veil, and even the priests do not go closer to it than the inner room. So at Shiloh I think it must have been kept inside a screen in the shrine, for it is clear that Samuel slept in the shrine also, to look after the Holy Lamp. Even Samuel, Blessed by God, could not sleep close to the Ark without a screen, I think. It would not be safe . . .

At any rate Samuel was lying on his cot one night when he was woken by a voice calling his name.

"Samuel! Samuel!"

He got up and ran to the little room beside the shrine where Eli slept.

"You called me, my lord," he said.

"What? Who's that? Samuel? Called? No, no, you were dreaming."

Samuel went back and lay down on his cot, but almost at once he heard his name called again, loudly and firmly, an unmistakable sound. At once he got up and went back to Eli.

"My lord, you did call," he said.

"No. Not I. Go and lie down."

So Samuel went back to his cot, faint-lit by the holy flame, while Eli lay in the unchanging dark of blindness and considered the wickedness of his own sons and the quick and honest love of Samuel. He was almost expecting Samuel to return once more, and this time he knew what to say. So it happened.

"I am sure you called my name, my lord."

"*I* did not call, Samuel. You heard a voice but it was not mine. You know Who else is in this place. Lie down again, and if you hear your name called, answer."

"My lord, my lord, I do not know what to say!"

"Say 'Speak, O God. I am your servant, listening.'"

And so it was. Samuel lay in that holy place, shuddering with the knowledge of the nearness of God, when his name was called again. He whispered the answer Eli had taught him, then listened to the message he was given. He did not sleep again that night.

In the morning, when he was helping the old priest rise and dress and prepare himself for the day, Eli said to him, sudden and sharp, "Well, boy, have you no word for me?"

Samuel began to stammer, but Eli reached out and took him by the shoulder and gripped him hard.

"Tell me," he said. "If you have a word for me and do not give it, God will do worse for you than anything he plans for me."

Samuel could hardly speak.

"My lord," he muttered. "It is because of your sons . . ."

"I know about my sons," said Eli. "They are my sons. What can I do?"

There was a silence. Suddenly a voice spoke. It was not Samuel's voice, though it came through his mouth. Nor was it his own mind that made the words. A power—the power that broods around the Ark, had gathered itself into him, funnelled through him and become language.

"A time is near," said the voice. "A thing will happen such that hearing it will be fire in the ears of Israel. In that day all the family of Eli will be destroyed for ever."

Then blind old Eli bowed his head and said, "It is the word of God. Let Him do whatever seems good to Him, for it will be good."

Is that the end of the story? Who thinks that is the end? Well, you are wrong. Who knows what did happen next? A battle, yes. No, we did not smash the Philistines in a great battle, far from it. No, none of you knows the true story, so will you please forget anything your fathers may have told you, and listen. While you are listening remember that it all came about because of two bad priests. A bad man is a bad man and a sorrow to his family. But a bad priest is still a priest, and the power of God flows through him. That power is danger-ous, even when a good priest is its tool. But when it's a bad priest . . . A bad priest, I tell you, is a disease at the heart of the people. Remember this, you will one day be priests!

The battle, yes, I'm coming to that. There were two battles. In the first the Philistines came out with their army to Aphek and the warriors of Israel gathered and fought them there and Israel was routed. Many honest and brave men died and the rest fled into the hills. That night there was sorrow and despair in the camp, with each man asking his neighbour why God had allowed such a thing to happen to His people.

"He was not with us," they said. "He was sitting in His shrine at Shiloh."

(See how little men understand about God! Does God sit in a house? Is He not everywhere, all at once?)

They sent to Shiloh, and Eli's sons, those two bad priests, hauled the Ark out of the shrine and set it on the shoulders of eight priests and carried it to Aphek. Eli's sons went too—the priests of the God of Battles could claim a good share of the booty after the victory.

When the Ark was carried into their camp, the soldiers of Israel raised a shout so loud that the Philistines heard it in their camp on the far side of the valley, and trembled. They knew it meant a great power had come into the army of Israel. But it made no difference. God did not allow the power to work, though He is the God of Battles. Next day the armies fought again, and again the soldiers of Israel ran from the field leaving their dead behind them. Among those dead were the two sons of Eli. And among the booty was the Ark of the Covenant of Israel.

All this while Eli was waiting, along with the old men and the women, at the Gate of the town of Shiloh for news of the battle, and of his sons, and of the Ark. He remembered the word which God had spoken through the mouth of Samuel, and his heart was dull with despair for his sons, as well as for Israel. But would not God save His own Ark? Surely. Surely.

Towards nightfall a man came running from the north. The people of Shiloh crowded out to meet him leaving old Eli helpless, sitting on a stone by the gateway. He heard a sudden wailing, louder and spreading as the news spread. He plucked at the air and called and called for someone to tell him what had happened. At length they brought the messenger to him, and the man flung himself flat in the dust of the gateway and cried out, "Israel is vanquished! Your sons are dead! The Ark is captured!"

Then that good old man stood up and cast his blind face to heaven and raised his arms. He stood thus for a while, like a young priest praising God, but before he could speak he fell backward. His neck struck the corner of the stone where he had been sitting and was broken. So Eli died. The word which God had spoken through Samuel had been made true.

That is all.

What happened to the Ark? How did it come here to the Temple? What? How? Did your fathers teach you nothing except how to ask questions? I will tell you some other time, because those are other stories. But now, remember this: a bad priest is a disease at the heart of the people.

There is one smaller thing you will be wise to remember. You may think you hear a voice calling your name in the middle of the night, and you may take it into your head to come and ask me if I called you, and I shall say "No." You may then decide it must have been God calling your name. Perhaps it will be so, perhaps not—I have a way of settling the question. I keep a cane by my bed, and with it I thrash any boy who comes to me in the night with such stories, thrash him until he howls. If he is lying he will tell me, and he will have been justly punished. But if he *did* hear a voice—it hasn't happened yet— he will tell me that also and no harm will have been done, because those who serve God must learn to suffer a little.

BETH SHEMESH

*Told during the haggling over a sale of land near the Western borders of
Israelite territory. Period of the Northern Kingdom, about 800 BC.*

◆

Seventy silvers! Ridiculous! You mock me! I tell you it is a prime field! I would
not take three hundred silvers for it! It is all good earth, two crops a season
and sometimes three! Every plant knows that God has laid a special blessing
on it!

That patch by the boundary stone? Good earth too. But it's holy ground, so
I don't till it or crop it, of course. But I tell you the sheep I graze there are fat
and healthy and always bear twin lambs—didn't I say it is all blessed by God?
Worth two hundred and eighty silvers at least! At least!

No, of course not. God Himself! The One God—not some trashy local Baal.
Where have you been living, not to know the story of the field of Joshua at
Beth Shemesh—this very field? Sit down, and I will send my son for a skin of
ewe's milk and you can drink and consider while I tell you the story. (Tell
your mother fresh milk, boy, from the ewe with the patched shoulder.) Now
sir, you must know what you are buying, and then you will no longer talk in
stupid sums.

Ninety silvers! Pfuh!

At least you must have heard of the battles at Aphek? You know how the
tribes were routed and the Ark of God taken? Good. Well, after the battles the
Philistines, poor fools, took and carried the Ark down to Ashdod, down this
very road, singing and dancing as they went. They put the Ark in the temple

of Dagon down there, in front of a big statue they had there. They used to worship this statue—they were heathens, of course—and they put the Ark down in front of it just like any other bit of booty, to do this god-thing honour.

In the middle of the night all Ashdod was shaken by a noise like thunder, and when the priests came into the temple next morning they found their god-thing lying flat on its face in front of the Ark.

They propped it back into place, but the same thing happened next night, only this time the god-thing had lost its arms and legs. I don't know what they did then—patched the god-thing together and put the Ark in a side-room, I should think. Heathen never learn.

Next all the people in Ashdod came out in lumps. Not ordinary boils, like you and I might get, but strange great swellings that itched and stank. At the same time all the town filled with mice—huge mice, almost as big as rats, and bold as leopards. Even the dogs were shy of them, and no wonder. The mice fought back, and where they bit the bites didn't heal.

I was wrong about heathen never learning. The people in Ashdod worked out in a couple of months what was causing the trouble, so they sent to Gath saying it was time one of the other cities had the honour of housing the Ark. They sent the Ark itself with the message, in case the people in Gath should turn it down. So it wasn't more than a day or two before the people of Gath were itching and stinking and the streets of Gath were swarming with monster mice, and the Prince of Gath was sending envoys to Ekron offering them the honour. And so on, until there wasn't a city in Philistia that would take the Ark.

That lasted all summer. About seven months after the battles at Aphek the Philistines did what they should have done in the first place. The Five Princes called their cunning men together and asked them how to get rid of the mice and the swellings.

"Send the Ark back to Israel," said the cunning men.

"Is that all?" said the Princes.

"No," said the cunning men. "You'll have to send a gift with the Ark, to show you did wrong in taking it. You should have left it where you found it among the dead at Aphek. Now each of you must tell his goldsmith to make him a golden mouse, and also a golden copy of one of these swellings that afflict us, and send them back with the Ark. That way the God of the Israelites will take back with Him the plagues He brought to us."

"It's a lot of gold," said the Princes.

"True," said the cunning men. "But you have no other use for it. You cannot lay it on your swellings to make them go away. You cannot put it out as bait for the mice, to poison them. What else matters to you now?"

"If we could be sure of what you say," said the Princes. "But how shall we know we are doing the right thing? Fools we'll look if we send all that gold to the Israelites and still don't get rid of the plagues."

"You will know," said the cunning men. "Your carpenters will make a brand new wagon, and your herdsmen will choose you two perfect white oxen which have never pulled a cart. You will put the Ark and the gold into the wagon and yoke the oxen up without any driver. If the oxen go wandering about, you will know the plagues have nothing to do with the Ark and you can take your gold back. But if the God of the Ark brought them on us because He wants to go home, you will see something else."

So it was done, exactly as the cunning men had advised, and for once they were right. God must have whispered to them, heathen though they were. As soon as the oxen felt their halters free they swung round, heading straight across the Ashdod Plain towards the highway—this same highway here. The five Princes and thousands of Philistines followed them, to see what would happen. The oxen turned along the highway and pulled steadily towards the hills. When they reached the boundary where our lands began—you can't see it from here—it's a dry canyon beyond that ridge—the oxen began to bellow. The Philistines stopped there, but the oxen came on. The people working those fields heard the bellowing and looked up. They saw a great army of Philistines gathered beyond the border, but before they had time to run for the hills they saw the wagon, all covered with garlands, and the Ark on top of it with its carrying-poles through the rings. Then they shouted and ran to greet it with songs and dances, and followed it all the way up the road until the oxen stopped of their own accord at this very spot, beside the tall stone there, which marks the boundary between my fields and Hophni's.

The people lifted the Ark reverently down and laid it in the centre of that patch, the one you asked about. They put the gold things on a cloth beside it. They broke the wagon up and made a fire in front of the stone, and there they sacrificed the oxen to God, on that very spot. That is why the land is blessed, and . . .

Hophni? Don't you listen to anything Hophni tells you! He's a liar and a fool! The Ark rested on *my* side of the stone. It was on Hophni's side that seventy men fell dead. God struck them dead because they had tried to look and see what was inside the Ark. Hophni's field is cursed—yes, cursed, so that his crops are always stunted and Hophni himself is a little mad.

But *this* field is blessed by the presence of the Ark, and though it is not large—but bigger than it looks from here, my friend, quite a bit bigger than you'd think—it is certainly worth every penny of two hundred and sixty silvers . . .

FIVE
THE ROAD TO JERUSALEM

HE FOUNDING OF THE KINGDOM—
1020–925 BC. The first King, Saul, is chosen by Samuel to lead the people against the Philistines. David replaces him, defeats the Philistines and establishes an empire with Jerusalem at its centre. Solomon succeeds, and builds the First Temple at Jerusalem.

DAVID AND GOLIATH

Told by a sergeant in the Babylonian army, training recruits in weapon drill. Period of the Exile, about 580 BC.

Stand at . . . ease!

Sta-and . . . easy!

Chew nut if you want, lads.

Right, what we're going on with this morning is Use of the Shield against the Sling. This ain't a tactic as you'll find yourselves having to use often, but you've got to know about it, case you ever find yourselves drafted for a punitive raid into sheep country.

Did I hear someone say *What's so bad about sheep?* Nothing, lad, till you want to nobble a flock for booty and they don't fancy going the way you're going. But it's not sheep you've got to watch out for, it's shepherds! Fellers from rough hill country, what've been driving off foxes and jackals—bears, even—from their flocks all their lives. Shepherd loses an animal and he'll have to pay his master for it, unless he can show him the carcase of the animal that took it. Right?

Now, see where the banner's set up outside the Captain's tent? How many javelin throws would you reckon to reach that in?

Two! Don't be stupid! That's three and a quarter throws by a javelineer, first-class! None of you lot'd reach it in five, except perhaps Lefty there. Now, suppose you was standing in javelin-throw of that there banner, aiming at the pole, how often would you hit it in five shots? Not once, none of you—and

112

that includes you, Lefty, so stop grinning. But a shepherd what's handy with his sling would hit that pole five times out of five, close range. From here . . . oh, twice out of five, maybe.

So that's the first thing you've got to get into your heads. A sling's got five times the range what a javelin has, and getting on five times the accuracy. What it's *not* got is the weight, and that's what gives you your chance against a slinger.

Provided. You. Know. How. To. Use. Your. Shield!

Right. Now I'm going to tell you a story as isn't in the manual, but it's as good an illustration as you could ask for how *not* to tackle a slinger. Eight years back I was on prisoner-escort, marching home from taking Jerusalem. I got talking with one of them Hebrews—we'd had one hell of a siege, starving them out—and he was trying to tell me that starving as they were we'd still not have taken Jerusalem if they'd had a couple of hundred fellers like David on the walls.

David? I say. Who's David? This is what he tells me.

Long time back the Hebrews were nothing but a pack of wild tribes in the hills. Then they started having trouble with their neighbours, a lot called Philistines, lived down on the coast, a notch or two more civilised than the Hebrews by the sound of it. Trying to get a bit of discipline into the tribes, the Hebrews chose themselves a King, big feller called Saul, and he put an army of a sort together and caught the Philistines two or three times unexpected. Naturally the Philistines wanted to put a stop to that, so they sent a real army up into the hills, teach the Hebrews a lesson, show them who's master. They didn't just go burning and looting, the usual way—they made a real propaganda effort. They'd got hold of a professional soldier, a giant of a man, nine feet tall my Hebrew said. His armour weighed as much as what I do, and you'd have had a job even to lift his javelin. Ruddy great shield, too, big as a door.

The Philistines manoeuvred around till they'd got the terrain they wanted for the exercise, a shallow valley with the armies drawn up on opposite slopes and a nice big space in the middle, so everybody had a good view. Then they sent the giant out in front of the battle-line, with his shield-bearer toddling beside him, and the giant strode up and down yelling at the Hebrews to send a man out to fight him. Just as you'd expect, nobody durst, and things were looking bad for King Saul. You see, a wild army like that, first and foremost it's a question of morale. They can do anything provided they're winning— I've seen a tribal charge get in among seasoned troops and wipe them clean off the battlefield—but as soon as they're losing they're no use at all. They just melt away. So that was the Philistine tactic—keep the giant parading up and down challenging them to come and fight till they start slipping back to their farms and then where's King Saul's army?

So Saul was at his wit's end when who says he'll take the giant on, but his own minstrel, lad called David? That's another thing about shepherds—sitting out alone on the hills all day they get handy with little home-made harps, or reed pipes, or some such. Keep themselves happy. This David had been doing a bit of that, or rather keeping the King happy when he was down, but now he said he'd take the giant on.

King Saul was so desperate he'd try anything. He wanted David to wear the King's own armour, look a bit impressive in front of the troops, at least, but that wasn't David's idea. Next morning David took his sling and went and chose himself a few pebbles out of a dry river bed, a bit heavier than what he'd use for jackals and such. He wasn't going to need the range, see? It was the weight what mattered. I dare say he took a couple of practice shots. I would.

Now, I want you to imagine you're this giant, parading up and down in front of the battle line, yelling at the savages to send somebody out to fight you. Last three days nobody's come and it's getting a bit monotonous. Then, all of a sudden there's this little feller coming towards you, not a sign of a weapon on him, not a scrap of armour. Right shoulder bare.

Mistake number one. You don't recognise him for a slinger. Bare right shoulder—that's the giveaway.

You can't believe he's serious so you shout to scare him off. He shouts back and comes on, so you go and meet him.

Mistake number two. You make yourself a target. Against slingers the rule is Stay In Rank. Move forward, yes, on command—shorten the range till you can get the javelins going. But . . . Stay. In. Rank!

You're still this giant, remember, and perhaps you're not so thick you don't guess the little feller's going to try and chuck something at you, so you take your shield from your shield-bearer, who's glad to get rid of it.

Mistake number three. Wrong sort of shield. Big as a door, didn't I tell you? Now this here's the right sort of shield—Babylonian Standard Issue—just the job against slingers, big enough to cover the head and neck, light enough to whip into place and out. Point is, a slinger always aims at the head. Sling-shot's never got the weight to get through armour. Right? So all you've got to guard is the head.

Now mistake number four comes back to mistake number one, and what was that? Recognise your enemy, wasn't it? Know what he's likely to get up

to. But you're this giant, blundering forward wearing armour as heavy as a man, with your great clumsy shield on your arm and your great clumsy spear in your hand. Are you watching what the little feller's up to? No, you're not. All you're thinking of is getting close and smashing him to jelly. He's running towards you, but all of a sudden he stops and strikes a pose . . . so! Look at me, lads! Legs well apart, see? Torso swung round so his left shoulder's pointing dead at you . . . so! That's how you can tell it's *you* he's aiming at, and not some feller five along in the rank. His right arm goes back. You can see that little jiggle of his wrist where the sling's spinning round. You won't see the sling—it's moving too fast. Now his right arm whips over . . . so!

Up with your shield! Clang!

Backward angle on the shield, see, glance the shot upward, not down onto your feet or sideways into your next-door's face. Then, soon as you hear that lovely clang, down shield so you can watch what the beggar's doing next. Easy as husking lentils when you've got the hang of it.

But did our giant know any of this? Did he hell. There he was, barging forward, shield down, bellowing his challenges, when David's first stone caught him slap in the middle of his great thick forehead. Not thick enough poor feller. Down he went like a tower falling in a siege and David ran up and whipped the giant's own sword out and hacked his head off.

Mind you, it wasn't only the death of the giant. Look what happened to the propaganda drive. The Philistines see their champ in all his armour carved up by a little Hebrew without any weapons at all—and the Hebrews see it too. Before the Philistines have got over the shock the tribesmen are coming at them in a whirling mob. No time to form rank, go into defensive drill, because now the tribesmen are in among them . . . and that was one punitive strike what got punished and struck.

Right! Spit your nut out! Ten-shun! Shield-drill, anti-sling, by numbers! On the command *One!* . . .

THE SICKNESS OF SAUL

Told in a Jewish medical school in Alexandria, as part of a course on demonic possession. About 220 BC.

Good morning, gentlemen.

Today we move on to fresh ground. Hitherto the sicknesses we have considered have been caused solely by the Irrational Demons. You have seen a patient possessed by Palinoth. He covered his beard with spittle and shuddered and fell to the ground. I have described to you the effects of possession by Parbosheth, the howlings and snappings and running on all fours. These are symptoms as clear as a rash or a fever, because the demon concerned is too stupid to attempt to conceal his presence. He simply takes the patient's body over and makes it behave as he wishes.

Diagnosis of possession by Rational Demons is an altogether more difficult task. It may therefore surprise you that we are going to begin with the Demon Rakah, who presents problems unusual even in this class. The reason for choosing Rakah is, however, simple. You are all acquainted with a classic case of possession by this demon — not personally acquainted, so you can stop looking nervously at the gentlemen on either side of you. I refer, of course, to the Sickness of King Saul, as told in the First Book of Samuel. I will now recount this well-known story, paying special attention to the medical aspects.

The first point to observe is that Saul was a strong, healthy, quick-tempered but naturally generous man. He had no history of sullenness or suspicion.

Second, he was under continual stress, leading a small and poorly armed nation against a stronger and better equipped enemy. Third—and I emphasise this—his life for a long while had been peculiarly fortunate. God had worked for him. From being a farmer's son he had come to wealth and power and glory. When such a man finds that suddenly his life is not running so well, it is peculiarly difficult for him to accept the truth, that God is working for him no longer. Instead he instinctively looks for other causes of his misfortune, and one such possible cause is a secret enemy. This gentlemen, is the moment of danger, the moment for which Rakah lies in ambush. It must have been in such a mood as this that the Demon entered into the soul of King Saul.

Now, I want you to imagine that in a very early stage of the possession—long before it is realised that a possession has occurred—you are asked for an opinion. A courtier tells you that he is a little worried by the King's behaviour. Arrangements are made for you to observe him without his knowing that he is being watched. What symptoms do you see?

First, in public—let us say at a law-giving. Nothing at all unusual. The eye perhaps a little sunk, an occasional sudden hunching of the shoulders, moments of inattention to the cases before him, or a point at which some detail of evidence is unreasonably seized on as an insult to the Royal Person. But on the whole a fair, even painstaking, law-giving, marked by a determination to look below the surface of the evidence, as if there might be secrets there.

Next, still in public, but less formal—say at a feast with his captains. Now a much more marked variation of humour. Watch the eyes for sidelong glances at a speaker without the head being turned. Silences, seeming refusals to hear a simple question, abrupt switching of the talk, snubs to old friends. Above all a marked leaning towards one or two of the company, almost a toadying on the part of the King, an appeal to the day's favourites for their love and trust. Put these together and you have clinical indications of possession by the demon Rakah.

Finally, in private, alone. This will be difficult. Rakah is ever on the watch for spies, but as you are now seriously perturbed you contrive the opportunity. You peep at the King, brooding in his tent, taut but listless. His eyes flicker from side to side. He mutters, starts from his seat, strides to the doorway as if to summon his scribe, stops, mutters, slinks back to his seat. If there is work, he does not do it. He sleeps sometimes too deeply to waken, but at other times passes his whole night in his chair, or keeping exhausted captains in conversation.

Always there is a sense of danger around him—danger to him, which he feels—danger from him, which he makes others feel.

You may now make a tentative diagnosis. The King is possessed. To confirm your diagnosis you instruct the courtiers to find a good musician to play to the King. It is an aspect of the demon's rationality that he appreciates music—so much so that it appears often to alleviate the main symptoms of possession. But at the same time you will be moving into dangerous territory, because if your diagnosis is correct the secondary stage is now approaching, in which the demon forces the patient to seek out the man or woman who is to become the partner in his suffering, a partnership as close as that between lover and lover, as bitter as that between torturer and victim.

The courtiers of King Saul were not aware of this danger. They believed they were merely soothing the King, and made the wrong choice, a single warrior, young and handsome, to sing old songs about fine heroes and clean battles and the loves of peasant peoples. If you read the Book of Samuel you will find discrepancies in the account of how David came on the scene. It does not matter. In my experience the patient meets his partner, his victim, by what appears to be pure chance. I can easily envisage one of the captains strolling at dusk through the camp and hearing a young foot-soldier singing the songs of home to his companions round a fire—true voice, clear eye, a sense of freshness—just the chap, thinks the captain, to cheer up the King who's been having these odd sullen moods.

And of course for a while the treatment seems wholly successful. Rakah sleeps. If he stirs, David is sent for at once to lull him back into his lair. But then his stirrings become more frequent, his sleepings briefer and briefer. David is constantly in the King's presence. He has become an obsession, an addiction. The partner has been found.

At this point, supposing you were advising the men round the King, you would become particularly wary. Of course you would some time ago have tried to introduce other musicians to the King, but very likely he would have refused to hear them. Now you would be deeply concerned by the fact that David has turned out to be a successful captain—naturally the King could not be prevented from promoting his new favourite—and also by his having struck up a close friendship with the King's son, Jonathan. For by now Rakah is only pretending to sleep. Night and day he is whispering in the King's heart. *David is stealing your glory. David is stealing your son's love.* Rakah is beginning to provide the patient with reasons for what will happen next. You will remember that I have already emphasised the rationality of this Demon. Here we see it at work. It does not matter that the reasons are untrue—we have every evidence, for instance, that Prince Jonathan remained a loving and dutiful son all his life—but they are good enough for the patient.

One evening, after an encouraging lull in the symptoms, you are told that the King has fallen into a deep depression and has sent for David to sing to him. You are alarmed. You remember the enthusiastic welcome David received from the army after he recently killed an enemy champion in single combat. You hurry to your watching-place by the King's tent. The sentries have orders to let you through. As you approach you hear David's voice, clear and triumphant, singing a song of battle and the glory of victory—ill-chosen, but here we have another aspect of Rakah's subtle power: somehow he contrives to act from a distance and influence the partner in the tragedy, so that the partner himself, from what seem to be the best possible motives, often acts in the very way to exacerbate the condition.

Well, you arrive at your watch-point. Through a slit in the hangings you can see the King's chair. He is sitting, hunched forward, chin in hand, glaring at nothingness. David is out of view but his voice fills the night. You observe with alarm that the King's weapons are stacked beside him, as if he were expecting a night attack. From the bunched muscles on the King's cheek-bones—these ones here—taut as the knuckle-end of a leg of lamb, you are certain that a crisis is coming, but before you can contrive an interruption the King leaps from his chair with a shout, snatches up a spear and hurls it. David whisks into sight, staring in amazement at the King, harp still in his hand. As well as amazement there is a look of calculation in his eyes as he measures distances—to the King, to the door. You read that look as the good warrior's calculation of his attacker's next move, but you guess that the King sees it too, and reads it less clinically than you. You can almost hear Rakah whispering in his heart. *David is stealing your throne.*

Another spear flies. David twists from its path like a dancer and is gone through the door.

So. The tertiary stage of possession has now definitely been reached. The object of excessive dependence has become the object of obsessive hate. If you had been there to advise, all your efforts would have concentrated on removing David permanently from the King's presence, but you would not have found this easy because to lay observers the illness would now appear to be cured. In more clinical language, Rakah has temporarily exhausted his powers in driving the King into overt action, and is now resting. Outwardly all seems to be well. The King apologises, begs David to forgive him, seems to want to prove that the attack was an unrepeatable moment of madness—indeed he offers him the hand of his daughter in marriage. Mark, gentlemen, how even in this phase of rest Rakah is still at work, gathering material for the next onslaught. What can David do about this proposed marriage? The offer can neither be declined nor accepted: to decline is proof of disloyalty, to accept, proof of ambition. In the end he declines.

But now we come to another of those "accidents" so typical of the way Rakah affects the course of events so that everything seems to fit in with his secret purposes. Though David manages to avoid the marriage to Princess Merab, what is he to do when Saul's other daughter, without any prompting from the King, falls in love with him? Can he now say no? But bow your heads and listen in imagination to the whisper in the heart of Saul. *He has stolen your son's love. He has stolen your daughter's love. He has stolen your glory. He has stolen the favour of God which once was yours. He will steal your throne.*

Now, rapidly and irrevocably, the possession moves through its tertiary stage, in which the whole energies of the sufferer are directed towards the persecution of the chosen partner. Even where the sufferer is a King, with armies to command and subjects to protect, everything becomes subservient to his vendetta. But observe how in the heat of hatred he is still at pains to provide himself with fuel for fresh flames. He arranges in turn for his son and his daughter to learn of a forthcoming attempt on David's life, thus forcing each of them to demonstrate, by helping David to escape, that David has stolen the loyalty which should belong to him, their father.

Our case history is drawing towards its close. There is nothing David can do. Neither protestation nor flight are any help. He hides himself in the remotest corner of the desert, but an army is gathered to pursue him there. By now the Demon has already effectively destroyed his subject. No public need, no social law, not even God's word can restrain the effects of the King's hatred. A priest gives bread to the fugitive, not having heard that the man is now the King's enemy. The King sends for the priest, refuses to listen to his case, and has him and his companions butchered on the spot. He sends swordsmen to the shrine the priests served, and they slaughter every living thing they find there, priest and layman, women, children, servants, cattle, the very dogs! And this is only exceptional in that Saul was a King and had the power to order it. Other men in the grip of Rakah, brave men once and honourable, have ended by perpetrating every last scrap of cruelty and vileness that was in their power. We are talking, sirs, of a strong and dangerous spirit.

Finally you must note how the case concluded. At last David withdrew himself beyond Saul's reach into the protection of the Philistines. He seemed by doing so to prove Saul's argument, that he was a traitor. But in its strange

way the partnership of hatred which this demon sets up is very like a partnership of love. When the second partner is removed the first can only pine. The
bond is snapped and he is widowed, with nothing left to hate, and so nothing
to live for. You know how Saul ended, broken in spirit before he was broken
in battle, and finally dying by his own hand. The terminal stage of this
possession is often exactly that. The patient takes his own life.

Such, gentlemen, was the case history of King Saul. I advise you in your
next study period to re-read the scroll and consider it in detail. Now we must
move on to possible courses of treatment. You will have gathered that in
dealing with a demon of the malignancy and intelligence of Rakah you will be
facing a series of very difficult decisions. First, then, the choice between herbs
and incantations . . .

SAUL AT EN DOR

*Told by the body-servant of the dead King, who has been summoned before
the new King, David. About 1000 BC.*

———

May the King live for ever!

The King wishes to know of the last days of my master, who was King Saul? Was it true that he had dealings with a witch, and that she bound him with spells so that when he fought the Philistines at Mount Gilboa he could scarcely raise his sword-arm?

My lord, he had such dealings, but they were not of that kind. Will it please the King to hear all I know?

My name is Cushai, and I was tent-servant to King Saul.

In his last days my master was very silent. Often he seemed to hide in his tent, and refuse to see his captains, though news came and came of the Philistine advance. He prayed for hours together, but God sent him no sign, not in dreams, nor from the oracle of the priests or the mouth of a prophet. One dusk, as I washed the King's feet, he spoke to me very suddenly.

"Find me a witch, one of the old sort."

I stammered. As the King knows, my master feared and served God, and worked all his days to root witchcraft and magic out of the Kingdom because of the Law God gave to Moses, which makes such things hateful. But he spoke the words again and then said no more. I asked among the servants of the camp and heard a rumour of a woman who controlled a strong spirit. I told my master, who nodded and said, "We will go. Order three donkeys—

124

not my mule. Do not say who they are for. Bring Jahdiel only."

Next morning the three of us set out—the King, Jahdiel his shield-bearer, who died at Gilboa, and I. My master wore none of his kingly ornaments but was dressed as if he had been a farmer, travelling with two servants. He would not stop to eat, so we rode through the heat of the day and came in early dusk to En Dor. I had not seen the place before, but as the words mean House of Water I had expected to find green trees by a pool with a shrine beside it, or stone huts around a rancid well. Instead we saw a narrow hill path leading to a cave, with a slimy trickle of a stream running down the rocks beside it. By the cave mouth sat an old woman, scrawny and poor and very dirty. As my master dismounted and walked towards her she asked for food in a beggar's whine.

"You have a spirit," he said in that soft and heavy voice of his.

She began to wheedle again, and say that such things were forbidden by King Saul.

"I say you have a spirit," he repeated.

"The King will send men to kill me," she whispered.

"As God is the only God, I say you will not be punished," he said.

She looked up and met his eyes. I thought his gaze mastered hers, but then I thought perhaps she was not unwilling to call her spirit—she liked to show her power, and little money can have come to her cave since the King's edict. She rose and hobbled into the cave. My master gestured to us to take the donkeys back down the hill, then followed her.

Jahdiel said to me, "One of us must know what she does."

My Lord, we loved my master, and we feared this woman, what she might do to him. My master was at times sick in his mind—surely my Lord the King knows this! Did he not suffer . . .

Very well, but may the King have mercy! I did not obey my master's wish, but while Jahdiel took the donkeys down the path I crept to the cave mouth. I could hear well enough, but I could see only dimly within.

There was a crack in the floor of the cave from which rose a thin, sharp-stinking mist. My master King Saul was standing with his back to me and watching the woman as she laid out a pattern of some small stuff—seeds, I think—on the ground. She spoke to the air in a strange language and threw more seeds into the crack. There was a little silence.

Slowly the woman, that old, bent creature, straightened her body until she stood stiff as a soldier of the King's guard. A new voice, the voice of a big man, came from her mouth.

"What is the task?" said the voice.

"Show me the ghost of Samuel, last of the Judges," said the King, unafraid.

Now there was a longer silence. My master did not stir but brooded at the dim-moving mist. Suddenly the woman collapsed back into her own shape.

"Why did you lie to me?" she shrieked. "You are King Saul!"

"What did you see?" said my master.

"I saw a great power rising from the earth," she whispered.

"What did it look like?" he asked, and for the first time for many weeks I heard a little warmth in his voice.

"I see him now," she said, whispering still. "An old man, covered with a cloak."

I could see nothing but the mist as it wavered up into the dark. But then as I peered at it it seemed to have gathered itself into lines that did not waver, though the mist continued to move through them. It was as though a man had been standing between the cave mouth and the crack, so that his shadow fell onto the moving mist—an old man, bent and bearded, robed to the floor.

A voice spoke. I could not see whether it came from the misty shadow or from the woman who was swaying like a drunkard on the far side of the crack. It was an old voice, bloodless, a dusty whisper.

"Saul," it said. "Why have you broken my sleep and dragged me up through the rocks?"

Then my master fell to his knees and bowed his head to the floor, as I am bowing before the King.

"Help me, Lord Samuel," he cried. "The Philistines have sent an army but God gives me no guidance. Why has God left me? I called you out of your rest to give me counsel, for the sake of Israel which you judged for so long."

"God is your enemy, Saul," said the voice. "I told you this day was coming. You made sacrifices which you should not have made, you kept booty which you should not have kept, you saved lives which you should not have saved. For this God has taken back the kingdom he gave you and now he will give it to David. He will never be your friend again. You will fight the Philistines and you and your sons will die."

My master groaned and reared up on his knees, arms spread wide, as if to implore the shadow, but it was gone. The groan became a long howl of pain and he fell full length on the floor. I ran into the cave. The fume from the crack was very strong. Perhaps that overcame him—and besides he had not eaten for a night and a day. I dragged him out into the open and Jahdiel ran to help, and we bathed his face in the water from the stream until he woke.

The woman would not take the King's money. Instead she scuttled away to another cave and brought out food, and we made the King eat. He said

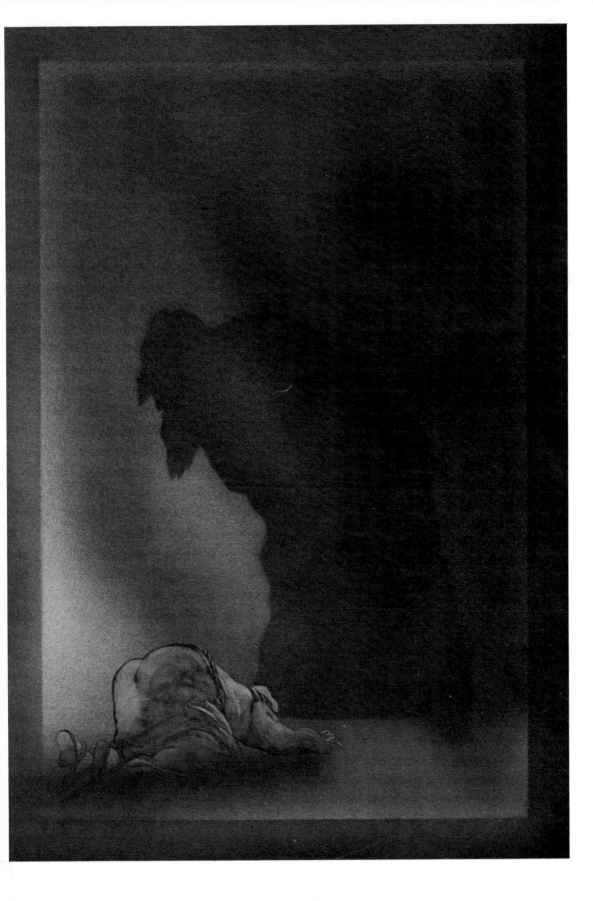

nothing. He looked strange, so that I was not even sure that he remembered what had happened in the cave. But he rode home with his shoulders squared, and called for his captains and gave orders for the advance to meet the Philistines on Mount Gilboa.

There, as my Lord knows, we fought. The King's sons were killed, and all his guard, and as my Lord can see I was wounded so that I could not stand. But even when all the army of Israel had melted away, none of the Philistines dared face King Saul hand to hand. They surrounded him with archers and shot at him, so that he was wounded many times. He ordered Jahdiel to kill him, but Jahdiel would not, so he set the hilt of his sword against a boulder and forced his body onto the blade, and then Jahdiel did the same.

But ever since we came from the cave my master spoke no word of what had happened at En Dor.

May the King live for ever! May the King have mercy on his servant!

ABSALOM

Dictated by an old man, a veteran of David's army and court, exiled to his country estate by King Solomon. 958 BC.

(Got plenty of fresh tablets, boy? We'll fill the drying rack before I've done.)

To Ahijah, son of Shisha, etcetera . . .

(Leave a space and put in the full formal greetings later.)

Son of my friend! You tell me that you have King Solomon's command to prepare a scroll, showing all the course of events that led to his becoming King, so that our children's children for many generations may know that it was God's will and his father King David's will. Since these events included the deaths of three older princes—Amnon, Absalom, Adonijah—and since I saw Prince Absalom die, you ask me for my account of that event.

You are just in time, my friend. There is death in my bones, though my doctor pretends to smile. Therefore I shall tell you exactly what I saw. The glory and honour of Kings demand that events must be changed if they seem to show them in an unflattering light, but I shall be dead before the King's swordsmen can come to me, as they came to my cousin Joab. Some of what I tell you you will know, but I include it to keep the thread of the story clear. Indeed, you may learn things about events you merely thought you knew!

I begin then with Princess Tamar. You will have heard of her but you will not remember her. No matter. How could you write into your scroll the grace of a walk, the sweet glance of an eye? But I saw her often, before the foreign custom of hiding young women away took so much of the pleasure out of

129

life. I have seen many fine men and women—Saul, King David himself, the Queen Bathsheba—but I have seen none to compare with the two children Queen Micaah bore to David, the Prince Absalom and the Princess Tamar. It was as if God had sent us a special sign of His favour, his blessing on Jerusalem, that such a pair should wander through our courtyards.

Of course you know what happened. Stupid Prince Amnon pretended to be sick and asked the King to send Tamar to his house to bake him some sweet little cakes. He got her alone into his room somehow and raped her and had his servants throw her out into the street. David forgave Amnon—after all he if anyone knew the force of sexual longing and the treacheries it can drive a man to. It was strange to us old desert warriors how freely David forgave people.

But Absalom did not rely on his father's famous forgiveness when he trapped Amnon at a sheep-shearing feast and had him murdered among the wine-cups under the pomegranate trees. He fled to Geshur and stayed there until the King grew so dismal with longing for him that it was safe to come back. We had an ingenious little intrigue to save the King's face. We hired an old woman to come asking for justice, telling a story that one of her sons had killed the other and her relations wanted her to give the surviving son up so they could take blood vengeance. Of course David, being David, found in her favour, and then everybody could say that if that was the law for her and her son it must also be the law for David and Absalom. David spotted at once we'd put her up to it, but he sent for Absalom all the same.

I was in court when Absalom came back, pretty as a doll, to beg the King's pardon for the murder of Amnon. The King came down from his throne and hugged him so that he almost lifted him from the ground. When he went back to the throne he stood and opened his mouth as if he were about to . . .

Oh my friend, how are you going to put into your scroll what it was like when David was moved by the spirit? Perhaps you never heard him—it happened seldom as he grew older. But when we were young, often—because a girl had caught his eye, because God seemed suddenly near, because one of us had fought well—he would stand motionless, gathering himself into himself, and then . . . then it was as though the air had become stone for his voice to carve on, so that the words would blaze there for ever! He carved on our hearts, at least. I could tell you the exact words of a song he made in praise of God's gift of fire on an icy night near Hereth, though I heard them just once, and that in the days when Saul was King and my beard was a thin fuzz.

(I've lost track, boy. What was I saying? Ah yes.)

. . . about to chant his joy, but no sound came. He sat down.

Joab, standing beside me, muttered, "We've made a mistake. Look at the Prince."

I tore my eyes from the King and looked at Absalom, so handsome, so tall, so kingly. I remembered he'd waited three years to murder Amnon. I wondered suddenly, suppose David had gone to that sheep-shearing, would *he* have lived?

So I took to watching the Prince, which wasn't difficult. He found ways of being seen. David was never a good law-giver—too hasty, too easily moved by someone's grief—and he knew it. He gave law as little as he could, but the people must have justice so they came to Absalom instead. He was careful to give law that would seem good to the men who mattered, especially anyone from the north. Then he'd take a chariot for even the shortest journey, and he began to have more and more runners clearing the way for him. And once a year he used to have his famous hair cut and publicly weighed, pounds and pounds of the stuff, as if to show there was so much life in him, so many sons in his loins. Oh, he hadn't wasted his time in exile—he'd spent it learning how the tribesmen think. He'd have made a good King, if he'd had the patience to wait. Of course David knew, but did nothing. All *we* could do was wait.

At last the storm broke. Absalom slipped north to Hebron and had himself proclaimed King there. The tribes marched on Jerusalem. We ran, and what a rabble we were! We took baggage and women and servants untrained in war. Even so we left half the King's women behind, and luckily for us Absalom was too busy proving his right to them to hurry after us. If he'd caught us before we'd crossed Jordan . . .

But he didn't. We made our base at Manahaim, far up beyond Jordan, and gathered our strength. Our army was four-fifths mercenaries, with no loyalty except to David. The rest were David's own clan. We were old, and dreary with the thought of another battle—the former days could never be renewed, even by bathing ourselves in fresh blood. The tribes when they at last came after us outnumbered us five to one—they were the old Host of Israel, the horde that had won the land, but with David's mercenaries to fight their battles I doubt if one of them had gone to war for a whole generation. We knew we would win, only there would be so much blood.

David took the salute as we marched out of the town. He'd wanted to lead the army but we'd overruled him. What was the point of winning the battle if we lost the King? Besides, there was Absalom. When David gave way over coming with us he sighed and looked round the circle of his captains.

"Deal gently with the Prince," he said. "He's still young."

So Joab was in command. I must say something about Joab. You will remember him only as a silent old man with a face like saddle-leather, still as lean as when we used to go raiding Midian in the days of King Saul. You will have been taught to hate and distrust him. Murderous, treacherous, more like a wild beast than a man, you will have been told. And yes, I saw him murder Saul's old general Abner, in the middle of a clasp of friendship, with a dagger slipped from his belt-fold and thrust up under the ribs. He had done many such things, I cannot deny it. And yet David not only forgave him—that was common—David loved him, and in his way Joab loved David. You would not have thought he was capable of love. But it was so.

Well, we met the tribes on the edge of that scrub country up beyond Succoth. We could choose the ground, because they would have fought us anywhere; so we waited for them with one flank against a broad ravine and the other against the wild country. We held their attack all morning, letting them lose heart. Then about noon Joab sent in his reserves on the right and swung the line round until the tribes broke, and there was nowhere for them to run except into the scrub. That's wicked country—they call it the Forest of Ephraim but there are few trees, just thickets and ravines and sudden slopes of loose shale. You can lose yourself in twenty paces. I should think the forest killed more of the tribesmen than our swords did. I was sitting with Joab in the middle of the afternoon, trying to make sense of the runners' reports—it was hard enough keeping track even of trained men—when one of our young officers came gasping up, saying they'd caught Absalom.

"Killed him?" said Joab in that flat voice of his.

"No, my Lord," said the man. "I heard that the King . . ."

"You've lost yourself a purse of silver and a sword-belt," said Joab.

He rose, jerking his head for me to follow. I went. I was numb with knowledge of what would happen, but I needed to see it. The man led us through tracks. The forest is a place used to silence, but out of its windings came sudden yells, horn-calls, the grunt and rattle of combat, groans and scrapings. We passed the bodies of many tribesmen.

The officer led us into a clearing in the middle of which stood a real tree, a single oak grazed flat beneath by deer. Absalom was in its shadow, erect in the middle of a circle of our men. I thought they had forced the King's son to dance for them until I saw that his feet were a handsbreadth from the ground and he was struggling with his famous hair trapped between two close-growing branches. Apparently his mule had bolted beneath the tree and he hadn't ducked low enough.

Joab strode up, unamazed. He snatched a throwing spear from one of the men and rammed it beneath the breast-plate, where the weight of the dangling body had opened up an inch-wide gap in the armour. Still with his face like a plank, he took two more spears and slammed them in, then turned to me.

"Back to work," he said.

As we left the clearing the soldiers were hacking the Prince's body to pieces.

The King had heard the news before we got back to base. A runner came out and told us that he was mourning in a little room above the gateway, so we crept exhausted into the town like a defeated army, instead of one that has saved a kingdom. Before dawn David sent for me.

I had decided to tell him that I had not seen Absalom's death, but when I came into his presence I found that my tongue would say only the truth. I spoke as drily as I was able. He paced the little bare room and when I had finished he stood still, gathering himself into himself. He lifted his head. The air prickled as I waited for the rush of the spirit, but when the King spoke all he said was one name, over and over and over. "Absalom my son. O my son Absalom."

This went on for a long time and there seemed no way it would ever stop until suddenly Joab banged into the room, limping with yesterday's effort. He was old too. We were all old. Before my face he gripped the King by both shoulders and shook him like a slave.

"What do you think you're up to?" he snapped. "If we'd died and Absalom had lived you'd be singing psalms! If you imagine Absalom would have let you live to sing them! We've saved your life and your kingdom but the work's not done. Unless you show yourself and praise the men who saved you, you'll have no army at all by sunset! Come on, man—show us you're still worth fighting for!"

That was more words than I'd ever heard Joab say, and the only time I'd seen him show any emotion at all. His voice was like a dry branch thrown on a fire—flameless in the sun, but you can hear the heat in the sound of it. He marched David down to the gateway. In the shadow of the arch he scrubbed the tear-marks from David's face with a corner of his tunic, then he set him on a dais and paraded the army before him. When they were all in drill order David made a speech, empty words of praise and thanks but in a clear enough voice and with his head held high. The men cheered. The towns-people watched. Joab sent messengers through the kingdom saying that David was still King. Then we marched back to Jerusalem.

That, I take it, is all you want to know. It is not all I want to say. Son of my friend, those of us who knew David in the old days . . . How shall I put it? There was a time when all Israel seemed to shine with an inward light, as if every man or woman you met had bathed in gold. Even our enemies were heroes . . . Saul, Jonathan . . . and when at last there was peace the light gathered itself into Jerusalem and streamed out again from there, the blessing of the Most High God on His people Israel. It was David who made this happen. Through him and because of him God gave us this glory. And then it began to fade.

Now, looking back, I can see the exact moment at which the fading began. It was when the Princess Tamar, with her long robe torn in two and the dust of the road on her shining hair . . . when she came staggering through the palace gateway sobbing for her brother, to be shut away, never to be beautiful again, never even seen . . . that was the spot from which the sickness spread.

But still the light was there, though tarnished. Some tried to use it—courtiers and such. Absalom tried to own it. Now King Solomon thinks he will make it perpetual by building a Temple of stone and cedar and gold. But some of us, especially the old comrades who hid with David in the wilderness and knew him then, tried neither to own nor use the light, and so God permitted a small share of it to live on inside us, unfading. I know that even as Benaiah's sword chopped into his scrawny old neck, my cousin Joab felt that light in his heart. And so do I. Perhaps you do too, but how will you put it in your scroll?

CITY OF GOLD

Told by a father to his son on the boy's first pilgrimage to Jerusalem,
on the crest of a hill looking west towards the city. About 700 BC.

You can open your eyes now.

There!

Don't say anything. Just look. I'll explain on our way down to catch up with the others—your business now is to store the sight away in your mind, so that you can remember it always . . .

Well, it's a family custom, I suppose. I don't know any of the pilgrims who do it outside our kin, but my father took me up this track and made me shut my eyes as we reached the top and led me forward by the hand, and he told me his father had done the same for him. I have found it . . . well . . . useful, I suppose. The city when you get there is so crowded, with the gabbling stall-holders and the jostling pilgrims and ten people in a room in every inn—even the Temple courtyard, though that's not so bad since the King threw out the filthy foreign idols and their priests—but yes, even in the Temple there's no *stillness*. Perhaps it's harder for us of the wilderness and the hills . . .

But . . . well, I've made this pilgrimage twenty-three times, and I still carry in my heart the picture my father first brought me up this track to see, the city lying gold and still along its ridge, the unchanging city at whose hub God broods in the dark between the cherubim. Even when I'm squirming through

136

the stinking crowd in the gate of the Temple, I can make all that seem as far-off and small as the buzz of a few flies, and find a stillness round me in which I can feel how close God is.

They call it Solomon's Temple, but it is ours. We made it. There are stones—I will show them to you—in its south-east corner which my grand-father's grandfather's grandfather helped to lever free from the rock-face in the quarry just above Geba. Then they split the stone, driving in wooden wedges and soaking them with water so that they swelled; and they man-handled the blocks onto sledges and dragged them with oxen to the city, where the masons sawed them to shape—but still we can tell our Geba stone because it has a pinkish flush in the gold. All the stone of these hills is soft to cut, and almost white when it first feels the air, but in a year or two it becomes hard and golden.

I have heard people saying that none of us Israelites were forced to join the work-gangs, that any who did so chose to out of loyalty to the King and love of God. They'll tell you it was only the Canaanites and other heathen who had to be forced into the labour. None of that's true. Every man in Israel joined the gangs, or paid someone else to take his place. One month in three they worked for the King—at the quarries, or dragging stone, or carting timber down from Lebanon. Anyone who tried to miss out on the work had his crops burnt by the King's soldiers, or his flocks driven off, or his house pulled down. Oh, yes, it was Solomon's Temple in that sense. But still, *we* made it.

Sometimes I ask myself how it can be that something we made—with our own hands and sweat, driven unwillingly to the work—there was an uprising in the Tekoa quarries, for instance, and the soldiers hanged eighteen men when it was over—how it can be that a building made in this fashion should become *holy*. I was talking with two young priests at the Temple three years ago, and one of them said that the building was like a great sacrifice, made by all Israel, but the other one said it wasn't the sort of question it made sense to ask about God. He started talking about what happened to Uzzah at the threshing floor of Nacon. You remember about that? No?

Well, when the Philistines were strong they captured the Ark of the Coven-ant, and after a while they kept it at Kiriath, which was in a part of the Israelite territory which they controlled. But when David had finally settled with the Philistines he decided to bring the Ark to Jerusalem, and he took a great procession of priests and people to fetch it, and white oxen pulling a brand-new cart. All went well for the first part of the journey, and David and the people were singing and dancing on the road, when they came to the threshing-floor of Nacon. Now you must know that nobody, not even the oldest priest, ever touches the Ark. It has two long carrying-poles set through rings on either side, and only the poles may be touched. When they came to the threshing floor of Nacon, one of the oxen stumbled and the cart skewed and tilted. Without thought, one of the men who was walking beside it, called Uzzah, flung out a hand to steady it. The moment his fingers touched the wood he fell dead.

Naturally enough David thought God must be angry with him for moving the Ark from Kiriath. He told the priests to lift it off the cart by its poles and set up its tent round it, and so they left it there on the threshing-floor. I don't imagine the farmer was all that pleased, until he saw how his crops grew that year and how his cattle fattened. When that news came to David he realised that the Ark still carried its blessing around it, so he came again and took it with songs and dancing to Jerusalem.

This priest I was talking to said that it made no sense to ask why God struck Uzzah dead, when he was doing, by instinct, what any man would do. It is in the nature of the Ark. It has that power. In the same way he said it made no sense to ask how a Temple built by the forced labour of a resentful people could become holy for that people. It is in the nature of God that often he blesses what seems to have been cursed and curses what seems to have been blessed. Mark you, the other priest was angry when he said this, and I left them arguing about it.

Yes, the Ark is in the Temple now. David kept it in his citadel. They say God would not let him build a Temple for it because he was a man of blood, so the task was reserved for Solomon who was to be a man of peace (I hope they explained that to the men in Tekoa quarries before they hanged 'em!) But when the Temple was finished—seven years it took to build—they carried in the Ark in triumph out of the Citadel, through the streets and up to the courtyard of the Temple. Beyond that, inside the building, is a great room where only the priests go, and beyond that still, up a flight of steps, is a smaller room where no man goes at all. There the Ark rests to this day, between the great six-winged cherubim, who glimmer beside it in the dark.

They say that while the people were still dancing and cheering and throwing garlands, and while the priests were still singing their hymns and sacrificing their thousands of beasts, God sent His sign. He filled the Temple with a darkness, blacker than night, thicker than smoke, so that the priests were like blind men though bright noon streamed down at the Temple doors. Then, slowly, God withdrew the darkness, gathering it into the inmost room. There is a curtain at the top of the steps, but even when it opened, and however many lamps the priests may have lit in the outer room, no eye can see one finger-breadth beyond the veil of dark at the top of the stair. Only the gold-bound ends of the carrying-poles of the Ark, and the wing-tips of the cherubim, glimmer at the edge of the darkness.

So God settled into His Temple, and from being mere stone and gold and cloth, which hands like yours and mine had shaped or woven, it became the most holy place in all the world.

I have felt it to be so. Not always. But sometimes, drawing a stillness round myself in the clamour and jostling of the courtyard, it is almost as though my soul were standing, eyes closed, by a great fire, whose heat throbbed out towards me. I do not need even to be there to feel it, because always I carry in my heart the vision of Jerusalem, lying in gold and stillness along its ridge, which my father gave me on my first pilgrimage.

Hew, what a crowd! The traffic on this road gets worse every year! We'll be lucky if we catch the others before they reach the gates!

SIX
PRINCES AND PROPHETS

THE NORTHERN KINGDOM 920–720 BC.
The ten northern tribes rebel against
Solomon's son and a separate kingdom is
formed. There the prophets of God
struggle to maintain the purity of worship against
Kings who for political reasons are continually encouraging alien cults. After long wars against Syria,
the Northern Kingdom is destroyed by the Assyrians
under Sennacherib.

Elijah in Exile

*Told by a pilot waiting for the tide in a tavern of a Phoenician
port. About 830 BC.*

———◆———

Afraid? Death? Not me. I've been dead once, and it was nothing to be afraid
of. Seriously. Look, there's a while to go yet before high water—buy us
another jar of the red, and I'll tell you . . .

Right. Mind you I was only a child, and I'm not going to pretend I remember every bit of it, what with my mother telling me the story over and
over until I couldn't say what she'd put into my mind and what was there
already, but . . .

You're too young to remember the Great Famine. No, not that one—that
was nothing more than one crop-failure—the Great Famine lasted three
whole years, with not a drop of rain anywhere all down this coast or the hills
behind, from Tarsus to Gaza. You'd have thought we'd have been all right
down here by the sea, but even the fish went somewhere else, and then the
salt began draining back into the wells . . . Why, we were paying for water
twice what you've just paid for that wine!

Times like that you get all sorts of strangers drifting along the roads—
mothers trying to nurse their babies back into life, men offering to sell you
their daughters for half a loaf, madmen preaching the end of the world or
babbling about some bunch of unheard-of gods who've lost their temper
with mankind, and so on. Now, my mother was out beyond the South Gate
gathering a few bits of firewood when one of these madmen came striding

up, so full of purpose that she thought he must have a message for her. (She never stopped telling herself my dad was going to turn up some day, spite of the whole crew seeing him washed overboard in a squall off Cyprus.)

"Bring me some water to drink," said the man.

Times like that you don't argue. You just turn and go. She'd got enough firewood by then.

"And a loaf of bread," the man called after her.

She always claimed there was something in his voice, but I don't know. More like her temper snapped—she had a brisk idea of matters at the best of times. So she started screeching at him how she was a sailor's widow, who'd been getting in enough wood to light the oven and bake the last scrapings of the meal from her jar with the last dribbles of oil from her bottle, so that she and her son could eat it and turn their faces to the wall and die. He stood, nodding once or twice, as though that was exactly what he wanted to hear. But even my mother had to draw breath some time.

"Do what I say," he said. "There is more meal and oil than you think— enough for a good loaf for you and your son and a little one for me. And my God, the One God, says this. There will always be meal in that jar and oil in that bottle until it pleases Him to send the rains again."

My mother, you'll have guessed, was by no means soft in the head—quite the opposite. When she went home she hadn't the slightest intention of giving the madman one crumb, but as soon as she set about her baking she found that there was a scrap more meal in the jar than she'd thought, and the same with the bottle and the oil. And then her hands, without her telling them, seemed to pat out a little loaf beside the one she'd meant to bake for us—not enough to do us another day, though. When the bread came out of the oven she cursed herself for a fool, and took the small loaf out to the madman with a cup of water.

Next thing, of course, he'd followed her home and she was cursing herself twice over for bringing an extra mouth under the roof. But within a week she'd changed her mind and decided he was a Man of God all right. He stayed three years.

Like? Children don't really *see* adults, not to describe them. I remember big eyes in a thin dark face. He was a southerner, spoke a dialect I could only make out one word in ten of, but my mother always seemed to get his drift. He paid no more attention to me than if I'd been a dog under the table—but then he didn't notice anyone else much, either. He sat in a corner of the room, mostly, waiting—not for anything in particular. Like a cliff waiting to fall, my mother once said. In fact he told her that his King had wanted to kill him for prophesying the famine and his God had told him to run up north, and now he was waiting for his God's next lot of orders. But . . . You'd have thought manners like that would have vexed my mother, who was always all taken up with the usefulness of things and people, and never had any patience with what hadn't got a purpose for her to see. But she put up with the madman very well.

Mind you, what he'd told her about the jar and the bottle was true. Somehow there was always another scraping of meal and another dribble of oil in them—though you'd have laughed at how it used to vex my mother, having to lean right into the jar day after day to scrabble that last cupful out of the bottom. If he'd filled it right up, she said, she'd still have felt on her honour to take only the top cupful off it . . .

The madman filling it himself, you mean? Sneaking meal in from a secret supply somewhere? No, I don't think so. Two reasons. Once when my mother was half way through baking, my father's cousin came in unexpected off his ship, and she went to the jar which she'd only just got the last bit out of and found there was enough in it for another loaf—*and* she and me'd been in the room all the time.

Then you know how boys are—I became inquisitive and I got a friend and together we rolled that jar right over and nothing came out at all. So we set it back in its place and I watched by the door until my mother came scuttling in and leaned herself right into the jar as usual, muttering with the effort, and scraped out enough meal to bake with. My bread was too sour for me to eat that night, but my mother swore she couldn't taste anything wrong with it. I looked at the madman but he wasn't paying any more attention than he ever did.

He came to us in the first year of the famine, I suppose. Towards the end of the next year I got sick. Children were dying all the time all over the town by then—no proper graves either—just a ditch they dropped the bodies in and filled up by digging the next stretch of ditch to take the next day's bodies. I must have fed better than most, but I was still a famine child, no sap in my marrow to throw off a bit of fever. Shivery at noon, coughing at nightfall, dead by morning. My mother woke and looked at me and set up the wail. Now, that was a noise the city was used to—you could hear it every morning, punctual, just like cock-crow, as the women woke and found their dead.

Of course she knew for sure! Hadn't she been helping the neighbours all those hot months, laying out the dead children, doing the best they could by way of a ritual before the barrows came for the bodies to take them off to the ditch? Middle of her wailing the madman came down the ladder from the loft

where he slept, and typically my mother worked him into the wail, saying that he'd come and brought the wrath of his God on her to punish her for some wickedness or other.

"Give me your son," he said, and he pushed the neighbour women aside from where they were bandaging me up in the grave cloths, and he slung me over his shoulder and carried me up the ladder with the cloths still trailing.

They didn't know what to do, so they just waited, listening to the madman groaning and muttering above them. The barrows came round but my mother sent them away. At last, long after mid-morning, the madman came down the ladder again—white as a dead fish my mother said, and dripping with sweat, but carrying me sleeping in his arms. As he laid me on the bed I opened my eyes.

Now I know what you're going to say, so don't say it. My mother *could* have been wrong, with me only in some kind of trance till the madman got me breathing again. Perhaps she could, but *I* couldn't. I was dead, and I knew I was dead, and that's one thing she could never have put into my mind, because she hadn't the imagination.

You tell me what you think being dead's like. Go on . . .

Well, you're wrong—it's nothing like dreaming. Just the opposite. When you're really dreaming you take your dreams for true, don't you? You live them, so to speak. Then you wake up and see what a parcel of nonsense they were—a few sharp pictures and a lot of misty foolishness. Dying's the same—like waking. All the scattered bits of yourself seem to piece themselves together and become a person—a *thing*—which is whole, in the way it was meant to be, and you look back on your life and it's all a lot of misty nonsense, which you can hardly remember at all. Only the last little bit—you know how it is with dreams?—that's still there. I was floating above the madman's cot, and I looked down and saw myself spread-eagled on it, with the madman on top of me, toe to toe, finger to finger, as if I'd been his shadow. I could see through the floor, too, where my mother and the other women were waiting round in the lower room. I wasn't all that interested. It didn't seem real. What was going to happen *next*—happen to this whole creature I'd become—that was real. The excitement of it was beginning to shudder through me when the madman hauled me back, down onto his cot.

So you see? What you and me are doing now, sitting in this tavern waiting for high water—that's nothing but a lot of nonsense dreams. It doesn't matter. In a dream kind of way I was glad for my mother's sake that the madman hauled me back, but it didn't matter either. And it's not going to matter what happens tonight. Suppose this rumour you've got hold of is right and they've started putting soldiers onto some of the trade-ships . . . well, for one thing they won't be ready for us. I'll bring you in out of the sunrise under her thwarts with the land-breeze behind us and you'll probably be able to slit the soldiers' throats while they're still snoring.

But supposing *they* catch *us*. Supposing they are awake and ready. What does it matter? Just keep telling yourself it's all only dreams.

Elijah at Carmel

Told by a priest of a Northern shrine entertaining a colleague from the
Southern Kingdom. About 730 BC.

———◆———

Prophets, my dear fellow? Yes, we have 'em. Don't you? No? You're lucky!

Oh, I don't know . . . one mustn't be uncharitable . . . certainly they contribute something, but . . . put it this way. Live and let live is *not* their motto. Still, they have something, they have something . . .

Tell me, has it ever struck you, when you are making a sacrifice and everything's going smoothly—knife sharp, skin flayed off with no fuss, organs all sound, fire going with the right sweet purr—has it ever struck you that for once in your life you would like it to happen as it happened in the old days, when the Fathers laid the offering on an undressed stone in the desert, and fire came from heaven and took it away?

You have? And do you think it's likely to happen with one of *your* offerings? Nor I mine—but it could still happen with a Prophet, I think . . .

Do they tell you down south about the doings on Mount Carmel, back in our King Ahab's time? No? One forgets how shut-off you are down there . . .

Ahab—now he was a King! Not one of your soft lurkers in palaces, but a man to command armies. Only a second-generation royal, of course. His father Omri had got the throne in a rebellion. But Ahab might have been another Saul—he looked a King and was one. And what's more he worshipped the One God—with a bit of give and take, of course, the way it is with kings. You can't expect them to toe the line all the time . . .

By the way, is it true what they're saying about this King you've got now? Child-sacrifice? Whew! No wonder you came north! I must admit we have a Baal-altar in an annexe to the shrine here, and an asherah, and we rub along with the Baal-priests, but child-sacrifice! You've got to draw the line somewhere!

I hope I haven't hurt your feelings, my dear fellow. Let's get back to King Ahab. Where was I?

Yes, he followed the One God most of the time, but his head wife did not. Queen Jezebel, came from Tyre, political marriage of course—she was a real fanatic for Baal. Altars everywhere, right *in* the shrines of the One God, cult prostitutes, four-fifths of the pilgrim-fees . . . disgusting! In those days there used to be a regular college of prophets attached to each of the shrines of the One God, and when they started complaining, why, Jezebel sent her Tyrian swordsmen into the colleges. Not many got away, they say, but one of them was Elijah.

He didn't go into hiding, not at once. He went and confronted the King, face to face, and in front of all the court he spoke a Doom. Prophets these days don't speak clear—it's all wrapped up in riddles, so you can't catch 'em out when the word fails to come true—but Elijah spoke his Doom clear enough. No rain for three years.

Being a follower of the One God, Ahab didn't have Elijah chopped on the spot, but as soon as Jezebel heard what was happening the swordsmen were after him. He ran away across Jordan—there's a quaint legend that the ravens kept him fed—and then he went north to one of those coastal ports, out of reach of the swordsmen.

Three years later he was back. One of the King's officers found him standing in the middle of the road, all alone.

"Send the King to me," said Elijah.

The man argued that the King would have him chopped for coming with a message like that, and made a lot of other excuses, but Elijah stared him down and in the end the man took the message. And do you know, the King came! I suppose he thought that if Elijah had brought the famine he could take it away again.

He found Elijah standing in the road where the officer had left him, just as if he'd never moved. The King leaped down from his mule and strode towards him.

"Your Doom brought this famine," he said. "You spoke evil, and evil came. I will have your head."

"I spoke the Doom that you prepared," answered Elijah. "The evil was your wife's and her priests' and prophets'. This I will show to you, and to all Israel."

The King had his hand on his sword-hilt.

"Gather the people, and these false priests, on Mount Carmel," said Elijah. "There let the test be made, and I will show you who is the One God. Only then can the rains fall."

The King looked round, over the withered plain. He saw the skeletons of beasts glistening along the roadside. He let the blade click home. Without even a nod of the head Elijah turned away.

I'm sorry, my dear fellow—one gets worked up, telling these old stories. I can see it all so clearly in my mind's eye; the delegates from the ten tribes gathering clan by clan on Carmel; the King rattling up in his chariot with his runners in front of him; the priests of Baal coming wailing up the track—you know the racket they make on a big occasion, with their tambourines and those rattly little drums—four hundred and fifty of them they say Jezebel had sent along; and Elijah striding alone up the slope, like a hawk among starlings; and over it all the glaring sky. You can see a long way from Carmel on a day like that and not a blade of green in all those miles, only the blue of the sea to the west and the roasted plain below.

Elijah climbed on a rock and spoke to the people.

"You are like a lame idiot," he told them. "A fellow that can't walk because he can't decide which leg to put forward. Either there is the One God and no other, or there are these foreign gods and no One God at all. Look! The King has brought here all these priests of the foreign gods, and I am the only prophet of the One God left alive. Is this a fair test? Let these priests prepare a sacrifice, only let them not light the timber to roast it. Instead let them pray to their gods to light the fire for them, and show that they are gods indeed. And when they have finished I will do the same test, and we shall see. If the One God can light my fire, then He can send rain again to your fields."

Of course all the people shouted. They needed the rain, but it wasn't only that. There was the excitement of the test, but it wasn't only that either. I think it was Elijah. Though I am a quiet-living priest who say it, I think he was a true prophet. He had outfaced the King in the roadway, and now he sucked the people into the vortex of his will, because it was the will of the One God. I like to think of him standing there, on one side, in his shaggy camel-hair coat and his rough leather belt; and on the other side all those Baal-priests in their gorgeous robes, with their musical instruments and ritual do-dahs; and the people not looking at them at all—only at Elijah.

So the test began. I expect you've seen 'em at it on one of their big feasts.

First they bring the ox bellowing to the pyre and kill and flay it in their unclean fashion, and piece it and pile the portions on the timber. Then, normally, they'd light the fire, but not this time. Then they start that circling parade—quite impressive when they really lay it on, I always think—with the outer ring going clockwise and the inner ring the other way—just marching to begin with and tapping their drums and chanting, then the march becoming a dance and the dance a convulsive leaping, and the chant rising into screams— and before long they'd have those hooky little daggers out and be slashing at their own arms and legs so that the blood streamed over them, mingling with the froth from their mouths. Usually they'd have the crowd with them by now—moaning and throwing themselves about and sticking daggers through their cheeks and so on—amazing what a pull some of those rituals have—I've felt it myself, so I haven't got it in my heart to blame simple-minded tribes-men for getting worked up. But it didn't happen on Carmel. The tribes watched stony-faced, while Elijah stood a little to one side, pretending to encourage them, telling them to shout louder and dance higher, because perhaps their Baals were asleep, or perhaps they'd gone hunting and were too busy to notice. So they danced and raved all morning until they fell exhausted in their double ring around the unlit pyre. King Ahab stood in his chariot and watched. I have it in my mind that he wasn't all that unhappy to see his wife's priests brought down a peg.

At noon Elijah led the tribes to the sacrifice which he'd prepared, a simple pyre with twelve stones set around it. He chose helpers and without a word from him they fetched their water-skins. Everyone watched while he killed the ox in the true manner, flayed it and piled the joints and entrails on the pyre. Then his helpers poured the water from their skins over the sacrifice and the pyre until the trench around it brimmed. Then everybody stood back and Elijah spoke in a clear voice, without any wailing or chanting, asking the One God to show the people His power, so that they should see and return to His worship.

By now it was nearly evening. The sky was the colour it goes in those drought-season sunsets, polished brass, with not a cloud anywhere. But as Elijah lowered his arms and his voice ceased, fire fell, lightning out of that empty sky, sheer onto the pyre. The sodden wood blazed like dry twigs, and the water in the trench boiled. Before the people had done shouting the sacrifice and the pyre were burnt away, and only the twelve stones were left, glowing with the heat of it.

By now the people were in a frenzy. It only needed a gesture from Elijah for them to close, whooping, round the priests of Baal and tear them apart, like a

monkey destroying a moth—all four hundred and fifty of them. Elijah left them to it. He had a look-out waiting on the mountain-top, and he came racing down with news of a cloud-bank building over the sea. Then for the first time Elijah spoke to the King—the test had been for the people, I think.

"The rains are coming," he said. "You will need to drive fast if your wheels are not to become stuck in the road."

So the King's charioteer turned the horses' heads and whipped their flanks. But the hand of God touched Elijah so that he was able to run before the chariot all the way to Jezreel, effortless as a loping deer. Seventeen miles they raced, and all the while the cloud-banks massed and darkened, and as they came to Jezreel at nightfall the storm broke and the rain streamed down on rejoicing Israel.

There! If there were prophets like that, these days, I wouldn't resent them so. Not that Elijah would ever have made a comfortable colleague . . . and just think of those priests of Baal, eh? Four hundred and fifty chopped in one afternoon—it must have made a bit of a hole in the hierarchy, don't you think?

ELISHA AND THE BEARS

Told by a mother to a small child, almost any period after 800 BC.

You're a nasty, rude little boy!

Do you know what happens to little boys who say things like that to their aunties?

THE BEARS COME AND GET THEM!

Yes, Holy Elisha's own special bears, whose business it is to punish rude little boys.

Because Holy Elisha was going along the road one day when a lot of nasty boys came out of their houses and shouted at him.

"Look at old baldy!" they shouted.

"Shiny-top! Wind blew his hair away! Go up you old bald-head!"

Then Holy Elisha lifted his staff and said a word, and out of the wood came TWO GREAT BIG BEARS!

And they gobbled up those rude boys scrunch, munch, crunch until there wasn't one little finger of any of them left. Then they went back into the wood.

Before Holy Elisha died he sent for those bears and told them they were going to live for ever, *provided* that from that day on, whenever they heard a little boy saying rude things to a grown up

THE BEARS CAME AND GOT HIM!

Now stop whining. It won't happen to you if you run off this moment and tell your auntie you're sorry. Otherwise I wouldn't care to be in *your* bed tonight!

At the Tomb of Elisha

Told by an old woman to her grand-daughter during an expedition to an area of cave tombs. Any time after 700 BC.

———◆———

This'll do, child. Help me down. Now tie the donkey in that bit of shade and I'll rest my old bones in this bit . . . No, we will certainly *not* eat anything yet! Can't you get it into your silly little head we're fasting? Perhaps we'll eat when I've seen whether Holy Elisha can do anything for me . . . Now listen—if you blubber you'll spoil it all, and we certainly won't eat in that case, so dry your eyes and I'll try to explain about Holy Elisha. What your mother's been doing, not teaching you these things, *I* don't know!

At least you've heard of Elisha's bears? I should think you have, pert little hussy like you, and I wouldn't be surprised if they didn't live round here, either. But you sit quiet and good and you won't come to any harm. What else? Well, Holy Elisha, he was one of *us*. He'd understand what it was like for an old woman who's ridden all this way because of the aches in her hips. He'll do something for me, if anyone will.

Why, he was ploughing his father's field when old Elijah came down the path and without a word threw his cloak over the young fellow by way of a sign that Elisha had to carry on with the God-work when Elijah was gone. (If any son of mine said he was going stravaging off to do God-work, I'd have a word to say to him!) And later on, when it was time for Elijah to go, Holy Elisha insisted on following him out into the wilderness. Elijah led the way down to Big River, where there was no sort of a ford, but he took off that cloak of his and

155

flogged the water with it and the river stood back so that the pair of them could walk across without even wetting their heels. Then they were going up through the wilderness when all of a sudden a chariot came down out of the sky, with winged horses to pull it, and all so bright they might have been on fire. Elijah climbed into the chariot and it flew away and nobody ever saw him again. He got whisked up into heaven, with no proper funeral at all, and no thought for his poor old mother who'd probably been waiting all those years to do the right thing by him. It's no use expecting God-workers to consider other people's feelings, I suppose.

What's God-work? I don't rightly know, child—there doesn't seem to be any of them doing it these days. It was mostly telling the Kings to slaughter all the Baal-priests and burn their shrines, or the Syrians would come and do for us. Yes, dealings with Kings and high-ups of that kind for the sake of the One God. You can't imagine old Elijah taking an interest in my hip-joints, apart from him not having a tomb to go to.

But Elisha, he was different. He was one of us. Oh, he must have been a God-worker all right, because when Elijah got whipped away in that chariot, the cloak I was telling you about came floating down from the sky and landed on Elisha's shoulders. And what's more, when he got back to Big River he took it off and flogged the water with it the way Elijah had done, and the water stood back same as before and he crossed over without wetting his heels. That shows he was a real God-worker.

But for all that he never got out of the way of doing little kindnesses for people, such as you or I might do for a neighbour if only we knew the trick of it. There was a well which had gone sour, but Elisha came and said a word to the water and threw some salt in it and it was sweet again. And another time he was walking by Big River when he heard a woodman lamenting that his axe-head had flown off and fallen in the river, so Elisha said a word to the river and threw a twig in it and the iron axe-head floated up.

What's more, he wasn't like these priests, always wanting a fee for every silly little thing they do for you. Not a bit of it! Why, when the Syrian King's top general came . . . at least your mother's told you about Holy Elisha and the Syrian King's top general?

She hasn't! I don't know what that hussy does with her time, honestly I don't! Didn't I warn your grandfather when he arranged the match? And now *I've* got to do everything for her. Well, there's nothing for it but to tell you from the beginning.

You remember those silver-skins who came to the village last month? That's right, with some of their fingers dropped off. And the men threw stones at

them until they went away. Well, the Syrian King's top General was a silver-skin, like them. *Leper* is the proper word. His name was . . . it'll come to me in a moment . . . Naaman. They ought to have driven him out, but I suppose it was difficult, him being the King's top general, and anyway you can't expect Syrians to know much about what's right and what's wrong.

Naaman used to come raiding down this way, and carrying off cattle and slaves, and one of these times he picked up a little girl about your age, and he kept her in his house as one of his slaves. But when she saw his horrible skin she said to one of the other slaves, "Our master ought to go to Samaria," she said. "We've a God-worker there who'd cure him as soon as look at him," she said. I suppose the slaves gossipped around till somehow or other it came to the ears of the King of Syria himself. I don't imagine he was happy having his top General a silver-skin, and he wanted to cure him, but of course he went and tackled things King-fashion.

We had a King of our own in Samaria, those days. I've forgotten his name, but the King of Syria sent to him saying, "Cure my General Naaman's skin, will you?"

Our King didn't take kindly to this, not he. In fact he went and tore his golden robe clean in two, to show how unhappy he was.

"Does he think I'm the One God?" he said. "Does he think I spend my time curing lepers? He's just looking for an excuse to come raiding again."

But by this time Naaman was on his way and there was nothing our King could do about it. But Elisha, being a God-worker, he knew what was going on and he sent word to the King saying he'd wasted a perfectly good robe, tearing it in two, because the One God had arranged all this to show there was still a God-worker in Israel, and when Naaman turned up our King was to send him on to Elisha. So that's what happened.

Just imagine. Elisha, he was one of us, remember, living in an ordinary house like your father's—just the two rooms with a flat roof, and a fig-tree beside the door with a goat tethered to it. Along comes this high-and-mighty general in his gold chariot, with his trumpeters and his banners and his spearmen in front of him and his slaves behind carrying all manner of presents for the God-worker—cloths and robes and gold and jewels—and Elisha won't even come out of his house to give him good morning. All he does is send a message out by his servant—remember the servant, child, because he comes in later—Gehazi was his name—he sends out Gehazi to say that General Naaman has to go down to Big River and bathe in it seven times. That shows what Elisha thought of your high-and-mighties!

Naaman, he was raging mad. He was used to being the most important person around, apart from his own King, and here he was being sent by our King to a common little mud house, where the God-worker won't even talk to him but sends him off instead for a bathe . . .

They soothed him down in the end.

"Look," they said. "Suppose the God-worker had told you to ride to the end of the world and climb the glass mountain and fight the dragon that guards the golden tree and bring back one of its apples, you'd have done that, or tried at least. It'll cost you nothing to try this river dip, will it?"

That's what they said, or something like it. No, child, I do *not* know if it was the same little girl who told them about Elisha in the first place, and if you interrupt I shan't finish the story. All I know is Naaman went off to Big River, still sulking I'll be bound, and bathed in it seven times and when he finished the flakes of silver were all washed away and the skin underneath was as smooth as a young soldier's. There!

Then, of course, he forgot his bad temper and drove back to Elisha's to give him all the presents he's brought. Only Elisha wouldn't touch them.

"This is not my work," he said. "It is the work of the One God."

Of course it isn't easy for a high-and-mighty to have his presents turned down, but in the end Naaman saw that Elisha meant what he said and drove away, vowing he'd worship the One God and the One God only as long as he lived.

But while Naaman and Elisha had been talking under the fig tree the servant Gehazi had been listening just inside the door. A little later Naaman is driving along the northern road, glorying in his new clean skin, when Gehazi comes running after him. Naaman pulls his horses up and waits till Gehazi stands panting by the chariot.

"My master sent me," said Gehazi. "Two young God-workers have just arrived at his house. Though he wants no presents for himself, these men are starving, and in rags. If the great General cared to give them something . . ."

Naaman can't refuse, can he? He gives Gehazi enough for ten young God-workers, bags of silver and several robes, and then he drives on north, while Gehazi sneaks home and hides all that stuff beneath his mattress. Then he comes out, as if nothing had happened, to give Elisha his supper.

"Where have you been, Gehazi?" says Elisha.

"Nowhere, master," says he, smooth as you please.

"Not so," says Elisha. "My soul went with you as you ran, Gehazi. I saw the chariot stop and wait for you. I heard what was said and answered. I stood beside you in your hut while you dug the little hollow in the earth below your mattress and laid the silver in it and covered it up. So now you have Naaman's silver, Gehazi. I will not take it away from you. You can buy yourself a house, and servants, and a vineyard, and a flock of sheep. But you have something else that was Naaman's. Look at your arm!''

Gehazi looks down and sees that the skin of his arm is covered with flakey scales, and the fingers of his hand are beginning to curl and wither. All over his body, head to toe, he was a silver-skin!

There! That's what comes of misbehaving when there's a God-worker around!

You'll remember that now, won't you, when I go into the cave. No, you silly baby, there aren't any bears in the cave. That's the tomb of Elisha, that is. And I'm going in for the sake of my poor old hips. Years after Elisha was dead and buried, there were some men who brought their dead brother out here to bury him in the family cave, but before they reached it they spotted some Moabite raiders coming, so they slipped the body into the nearest cave, which was that one there, and ran away and hid. When the raiders had gone by the men came back to go on with the burying, but they'd hardly reached this spot when they saw their brother come striding down the slope to greet them, live as could be! If Holy Elisha could do that for a dead man, I don't see why he shouldn't do something for my aches and pains.

So you wait here, and no matter how hungry you feel you won't go anywhere near that food we've brought. We're fasting, remember, because we want to do things properly, and it's not a clever idea trying to cheat a God-worker when you think there's nobody looking. Don't forget what happened to Gehazi!

SEVEN
THE STONES OF THE TEMPLE

HE SOUTHERN KINGDOM 925–587 BC. Apart from one brief interlude the descendants of David rule in the small kingdom, but often as vassals, first of the Northern Kingdom and then of Assyria or Egypt. Lying between these two great empires, the Southern Kingdom exists in endless intrigues. Twice attackers are bought off with Temple treasures, but in the end the last Kings go too far and the armies of Babylon, the successors of Assyria, destroy both city and Temple and take the Jews into exile.

ATHALIAH

Told by Joash, King of Judah, writing in his private day-room in his
palace in Jerusalem, about 800 BC.

I, Joash, write this scroll. I have cut the parchment to this odd shape, and write
as small as I can, because when I have finished it the scroll must fit into the
secret hollow I found in the wall of this room when I was still a child, though
already King of Judah.

I begin.

The first time I saw Queen Athaliah I was four years old. My aunt Jehosheba
took me by the hand and led me through many passages to a window that
looked down over the Temple courtyard. She lifted me up but held me well
back from the windowsill, so that the darkness of the room should hide me
from anybody looking up from the courtyard. I had never seen out of this
window before. All my life had been spent in rooms whose windows looked
out onto close little alleys, or sometimes over higgledy-piggledy roofs to
blue-brown distances of hills. Now I was staring down into a great space of
gold stone, so bright under the sun that I screwed up my eyes and turned my
head away.

"Look!" said my aunt in an angry whisper.

I peered through the dazzle. There were men in the courtyard, arranged in a
pattern of neat rows. They glistened, some with armour and some with priestly
ornaments, as I now know. All I saw as a child was men wearing piercing
points of light, too bright to look at. I had seen very few men before. Till then it

had seemed to me that women were the rule, and men the exceptions.

After a while the Temple horns sounded, nine times. As the last note died my aunt pointed. Out of the dark mouth of an arch came a procession—soldiers with spears, trumpeters, priests, men in rich clothes, and then four men carrying the poles of a gold and purple canopy—how often I have walked in procession to the Temple under that canopy! Beneath it was a woman, outlined in the shadow against the glaring pavement beyond. I could see how small and dumpy she was, compared to the tall soldiers and the tall priests, and in her thick robes she seemed to have neither arms nor legs. But even I, a child, could see from the way she moved that she expected all the others to be afraid of her. Before my aunt spoke I knew that I had been brought to the window to look at her.

"That is the Queen," whispered my aunt. "Your grandmother. Her name is Athaliah. One day, with your help, I am going to kill her."

Of course the words had no real meaning to me. She took me back to the little rooms behind the priests' quarters where all there was to see was alleys and roofs and far-away hills, and where women were the rule.

A year or so later a man came to see me. He wore a robe of purple and scarlet and gold, with a turban on his head. His face was lined like water-worn hills, and his eyes burned as though God had lit a fire within, but he told me in a gentle voice that he was my friend. He talked for a little while about such things as interest children, and then he nodded as though he had made up his mind, and left. It was several years more before I was told that he was my aunt's husband, Jehoiada the High Priest.

After his visit my aunt and the other women began play-acting—strange plays in which they took the parts of men, but I was always the King, and I had to learn my lines well and speak them clearly, but not so loud that they might be heard in another room. I never played in the alleys or went out into the sun. Time passed—as slowly as it does, I suppose, for all children.

When I was nearly seven the High Priest Jehoiada came back. He sent the women away, set me on a stool by his side and told me a story, using simple words a child could understand. He said there had been a King of Judah called Jehoram, and he was my father's father. He had married a foreign woman who worshipped vile gods. When Jehoram had died, my father Ahaziah had become King, but within a year he had been killed in a battle. Then the foreign woman had given orders that all my father's sons must be killed, so that she could be Queen and there would be nobody who could take the throne from her. The killing was done in the lower courtyard of the palace—I have made it into a garden, but I never go there—but my father had taken new wives when he was made King, and three of these now had baby sons. My aunt Jehosheba, my father's sister, managed to steal one of these in the confusion while the soldiers were collecting the small princes for slaughter, and she smuggled him away to the priests' quarters and brought him up there, and that was me.

Now, soon, the High Priest said, I was going to take my throne back and avenge the deaths of my brothers by killing Queen Athaliah, and drive her vile foreign gods out of the Temple.

I was not afraid. I understood about being a King. All it meant was that I stood up and said my lines clearly and made certain movements which I had rehearsed a hundred times. It was not difficult. But I was not sure how I was going to kill my grandmother. Her robes were so thick. Jehoiada the High Priest said that my soldiers would do the killing for me—it was all arranged. I frowned because I was not going to kill her myself, and he smiled at me.

A little after that my aunt came and woke me early one morning and dressed me in stiff new clothes of gold and purple which she had been sewing for many days. I could feel a special sort of silence in the women's quarters, beneath the flutter and scurry. When anybody spoke it sounded as though they would have preferred to whisper. I knew it was no play I would be acting today because they would not give me any breakfast. When they make you fast, it means they are in earnest.

Instead of breakfast my aunt read to me about Samuel anointing David King over Israel, and then about the coronation of Solomon. I asked her to read about Goliath, but she would not. Men in priest's clothes came and led me down to the lower floor—where I had never been in my life—and put me on a chair with poles running along the sides so that they could carry me on their shoulders. So, close against the ceilings and ducking where the arches came, I was carried along corridors and through small courtyards—once even through a great kitchen with no cooks but the ovens all warm. A priest walked twenty paces in front of us, and when he stopped we stopped too, once so suddenly that I almost tumbled forward out of my chair. The priest would peep round a corner, make a sign, move out of sight, and then we would follow him. In a few places there were armed men stationed. They saluted as we passed, but without stamping their feet or letting their spear-butts bang the ground.

I was carried into the Temple by a little side door. We waited for a long while at the side of the great central chamber called the Hekal. The darkness was lit by lamps and smelt of incense. On our right I could see the steps going up to the curtain which veils the Holy of Holies, where the Ark of the Covenant rests, but of course I did not know what I was looking at. Then they carried me down the centre of the Hekal, out to the edge of sunlight under the portico, and set my

chair down by the pillar whose name is Yakin. I stepped out onto the dais there. I knew just what to do, having acted all this in my aunt's plays. The courtyard was full of priests and soldiers, armed with strange old spears that had been taken from the Temple treasury. This I learnt afterwards—while the ceremony was in progress I was wholly absorbed, child-fashion, in acting my part as King. I did not notice anything outside myself until the Queen came.

The High Priest Jehoiada had prayed beside me and placed the circlet on my head, and I had answered with the words I had been taught. He had given me the Testament of the Covenant and I had accepted it. He had poured the sacred oil onto my scalp and prayed again, and I had answered again. Then he had changed my name—it used to be Jehoash—to my new King-name and proclaimed me to the people. The horn had sounded and the people had clapped their hands and shouted "Long live the King!" (There were not any *people* there—none of the people it is now my business to rule, I mean—craftsmen and farmers and merchants—only soldiers and priests. They did the shouting on behalf of the people.)

The noise went on for some time. It was beginning to die away when almost between one heartbeat and the next it stopped completely. I woke from my trance of kingship and looked to see what had gone wrong with the play, and there, standing five paces from me, was my grandmother the Queen. Her face was pale and old, but smooth. Her eyes were black, the iris so dark that the whole round of it seemed to be pupil, fiery but calm. A short, stocky woman in a simple brown robe, I think. I am still not sure. I can remember only those eyes.

She looked at me for a moment, not very interested, and I felt myself beginning to melt like a crumb of water-ice dropped onto hot paving. Her glance flicked towards Jehoiada, full of furious understanding. The whole courtyard was quite silent. She had brought no one with her. She had come at once from the palace, hearing the shouts and the clapping. She was one woman and they were many, many priests and soldiers.

Nobody moved until she lifted her hands to the neck of her robe and tore it from hem to hem. The rasp of tearing filled the big space.

"Treason!" she cried.

I have often thought since that if she had not spoken she could have carried it off. If she had simply cocked her head to summon the nearest soldier and then gestured towards the High Priest, the soldier might have taken his spear and run him through while we were all spellbound. But her voice broke the spell.

A priest slid forward from the rank behind her and clapped his hand over her mouth before she could shout again. Two other priests took her by the arms, but she did not struggle.

"Do not pollute the Temple with her blood," said Jehoiada in a slurred voice, like that of a waking man still half in his dream. So the soldiers took her out and killed her at the stable gates of the palace.

I climbed back into my chair. The horns blew, the men shouted, the chair-bearers picked me up, and making all the noise they could—as if to drive away the ghost of the stillness which the Queen had brought with her—they took me into the palace and put me on my throne, to complete the coronation of the rightful Heir of David.

I have been a good King, I think my subjects would agree. At first I did whatever the priests told me, destroying the shrines of the Baals which Athaliah had installed in the Temple courtyard, and suppressing the shrines elsewhere. Then I began to challenge the priests—they had been taking much more than their share of the Temple dues and letting the building itself go to ruin. There was trouble about that, but the One God has shown His approval by allowing me to be fortunate in my Syrian wars. I have ruled a very long time—longer than He allowed either to David or Solomon. But still I do not feel like a King.

No, I am certainly not a King in the same way that Athaliah was certainly a Queen. I could not by my single will compel a courtyard full of my enemies all armed, to silence.

This thought did not trouble me when I was a child, and very little when I was a young man. It is only since the business with the Temple dues—when I first saw how *wrong* the One God could permit His priests to be—that I began to wonder whether I am the Heir of David at all. My father's sons were known and numbered, surely. Athaliah, their grandmother, would be the first to be told of the birth of any boy. Would *she* have allowed her soldiers to make a mistake in the counting? There is no way I can check, no one alive I can ask.

My mother—I mean the mother of the baby Prince Jehoash—was called Zibiah and was killed on the orders of Athaliah. That I know. But do I remember, or have I simply begun to imagine, that when I was very small a strange woman sometimes crept into my room and picked me up and held me close, without saying a word?

Suppose you are High Priest, and suppose a foreign woman makes herself Queen by killing off all the male heirs to the throne, and then pollutes the Temple with the shrines of loathsome gods. You must drive her out, but how? If only you could find an heir, in the Royal Line of David, it might not be difficult. But all such heirs are dead. So you invent an heir. You find a child of the right age . . .

Can that have happened? Would the One God permit it, so close to where His Ark rests in its darkness? Jehoiada is dead. Jehosheba, who called herself my aunt, is dead (soon after the Queen, as if she had nothing to live for once vengeance was taken). They are all dead. I don't know! I don't know! I don't know!

All I know is that I am not truly a King in the manner that Athaliah was truly a Queen.

THE BRONZE SERPENT

*Told by an old priest living alone in an abandoned Assyrian siege-fort
on the road outside Jerusalem. 700 BC.*

Tsk! Such a fuss! And my poor old serpent smashed. I didn't know whether I
was on my head or my heels, really I didn't. Of course I can see it all quite
clearly now—only God works in such strange ways, doesn't He? At the time it
can be very confusing, very confusing.

You see the people were fond of my serpent. Not your nobles, not your High
Priests, but the cobblers and the coppersmiths and the farmers who brought
their vegetables in on market-days—when there wasn't a siege on, that is.
Moses made it, you know, and it was something they could see and understand. Not an emptiness on an empty throne in a hidden room which only the
High Priest could go into, and that only once a year, but a big, bronze coiling
serpent. Why, you could have touched it, if you'd dared! But even I, the priest
of the Bronze Serpent, never once touched it with my naked flesh, not once in
seventy-seven years. Think of that! And then ordinary workmen came and
smashed it with hammers and nothing happened to them! Of course I understand *now*, but at the time—I was very confused, but I remember wondering
why there hadn't been at least a grumble of thunder. No, nothing.

It *belonged* in the Temple, you see. It had always been there. It wasn't one of
those filthy foreign Ashtaroths or Cuthahs, with their painted priests and their
women in the booths behind the altars, doing I don't know what for the
worshippers. *They* didn't belong in the Temple! Certainly not! Disgusting!

Where was I? Oh, yes—I was really glad when the new King turned the Ashtaroths and the Cuthahs out, and had that obscene pole smashed—not that it had bothered me much in the last twenty years, since my sight got so feeble, but . . . Nobody likes to see a priest turned out of a job, of course, and I suppose they themselves sincerely thought they were doing the right thing, but you couldn't help wondering. Their language! And what they got up to with the sacred women when there weren't any worshippers about! Right there, in the courtyard of the Temple! No, I sang psalms in my heart when King Hezekiah sent them all packing.

But the King didn't worry about my serpent *then*. Moses made it, you see—did I tell you that?—so it was all right. Why they even moved it into a new place on the black obsidian plinth where the horrible pillar had stood, and everybody said it looked splendid there—I couldn't really see well enough, but I could imagine it—and nobody complained, not even the High Priest. You see, I never went saying that my Bronze Serpent was a god. It couldn't be. There's only the One God, isn't there? No, it was just a sort of holy thing Moses had made, and the ordinary people used to come with little sacrifices—meal-cakes or oil, mostly—and ask it to help with the sort of troubles they didn't like to bother the One God with—cure their sons of warts, or send a good workman to mend a leaky cistern . . . though I must admit there was a bit of superstition about my serpent helping girls find buried treasure for their dowries, but I never encouraged that sort of nonsense. Never.

The great thing about the Bronze Serpent, you see, was that it was cheap. I charged very little for a sacrifice. After all, it was the poor people who came to me, and my needs are few. Anything to spare I always put straight in the Temple Treasury . . . I don't want to accuse anyone, but I can't help thinking there may have been a little jealousy—a little spite, even. We were too popular for the liking of some of the priests, my serpent and I. After a few years they moved us off our plinth and round by the northern wall out of the way, but I didn't mind provided the people went on coming.

And then of course these tiresome sieges began. I must say, if I were King of the Assyrians I wouldn't go rampaging round besieging foreign cities. He must have a lovely garden and palace by that river of his. And in the end he didn't take Jerusalem at all. He smashed up the Northern Kingdom, and that may have given him some satisfaction, I suppose.

King Hezekiah bought him off first time. Stripped the Temple of gold and silver to do it. I must say, I was glad my poor old serpent was only bronze. Then was it next time? . . . No, next time the Assyrians came and made a lot of threats and went away again. It was the *third* time . . . yes, that's right . . .

It was a real siege—several months. I hardly noticed at first. A bag of meal lasts me longer than most people, and I'd never been very interested in anything that happened outside the Temple . . . and besides I knew the One God would never let His City be taken, so what did a siege or two matter? The sacrifices got skimpier but I didn't complain. Then, though, my people started asking the serpent to send the Assyrians away. Of course I packed them off to the One God for a thing like that, but I didn't see . . . I didn't realise . . . how blind I was!

They were coming to the serpent, you see, because they'd decided the One God wasn't any use! Poor silly children! And poor silly old man, flattered to think people admired his serpent enough to ask it to do a thing like that!

It was all terribly sudden. A great shock. I was at my little altar when a hush fell on the courtyard and somebody whispered that the King was there with the High Priest. My eyes aren't very good—did I tell you?—so I couldn't see them, just a blur of bright-clothed men by the Two Pillars. Then I sensed from the movement of my worshippers that the King was coming my way. I was terribly pleased—he hadn't deigned to notice my serpent since they'd moved it off the dais. Then I could actually see where he was, all gold and purple, and the High Priest green and red beside him, and I was bobbing and smiling like a monkey. Then I felt the stillness.

"That rubbish must go," said the King.

"It is an obscenity," said the High Priest.

"Thou shalt make no graven image," said the King.

Do you know, it was only then that I had the least inkling they were talking about my serpent! I began to mumble.

"But Moses . . ." I said.

"Superstitious nonsense!" snapped the High Priest.

"No wonder the One God is still angry," said the King in a loud voice, so that everybody should hear. "How can we ask Him to drive the Assyrians away when we let this sort of disgusting blasphemy take place in His very Temple? It must be smashed and melted down at once."

"It shall be begun this hour," said the High Priest.

"Smashed?" I stammered. "Melted? What shall I . . ."

The King was turning away, but he spoke over his shoulder.

"How long has that old fool been performing this abomination?" he said.

"Seventy-seven years ago I first . . ." I began.

"He must go too," said the King.

"He is deep in pollution," said the High Priest.

And I had sat in the same class of boy-priests as his grandfather! I had taught both him and his father the mysteries of the Bronze Serpent!

"Go?" I whispered. Leave the Temple, did they mean? After all these years? Didn't they know there was a siege on? Every hovel would be full.

The King turned slowly back.

"Old man," he said. "Count yourself lucky. Time was when the priest of an abomination would have been hewed to pieces on his altar and his bones used to desecrate the shrine. Even now I must pray that the One God will pardon me for sparing your life. You are pollution, and if you remain within the city you will pollute us all. Put him beyond the walls!"

I stood there with my mouth open, shaking my head, unable to say a word, until two of the Temple Guards took me by the elbows and led me away. As I went through the outer gate of the courtyard I heard the hammers thudding into my poor old serpent. Ah well!

I don't really know what happened next. Shock of course. All I can remember is wondering why there wasn't a thunderbolt. The guards must have led me down—or carried me—I don't weigh much, especially at siege-times—and then I thought I was flying until something jolted against my side—and there I was outside the walls! They'd let me down in one of those big baskets people use to bring vegetables into the city—one on each side of a donkey, you know—and it fell over when it hit the ground and tipped me out. I couldn't see to the top of the wall but I heard them laughing as the basket went swaying up into the sky.

Fifty-three years! That's how long it was since my nephew's wedding-feast at Bethany, the last time I'd been outside the walls. He's dead now, of course, *and* that fat child he married. All dead! Only me left, standing on a rubbish tip with the carrion birds settling down again—they knew I was no danger to them. Well, I thought, if I was pollution I'd be thrown out with the rest of the rubbish, wouldn't I? Kind of them to let me down in a basket. Almost everybody means well, in my experience, you know. King Hezekiah, for instance—I'm sure he thought he was doing his best for the city . . . And he was! He was! Only he'd no idea how God was going to make it happen!

I didn't really want to die on the rubbish tip, because of the smell. I've always had a sensitive nose—one of the reasons why I never cared for some of those foreign gods . . . It might take quite a long time to die, I thought, so I'd better go somewhere else. I expect I crawled more than I walked. It's lucky I didn't fall and break a bone, because it's quite steep there . . . yes . . . but then there was a little path going slantwise and I followed it . . . I was quite lost, of course. I can only see a few yards at the best of times, and with my eyes full of tears . . .

And then, do you know, an extraordinary thing happened! Sometimes I tell myself I heard a voice, but I can't honestly say I'm sure. It happens to some people, you know, when they're lost, and all hope's gone. Hagar, for instance—the angel of God spoke to her, didn't he, when Abraham had cast her out of his camp all alone with her son in the desert? Perhaps . . . at any rate, I was stumbling along that path looking for a place to die when a quite new thought blazed up in my mind, out of nowhere. *I am pollution. It is the will of the One God. He orders me to go and pollute these Assyrians.*

God must have guided me, too. Remember I had no idea where I was—I didn't even know if the city was behind me or in front. The path dipped and climbed, quite steep, but He gave me strength to follow it until I heard the squabbling and flapping of birds and the buzz of flies and I thought, Drat it, I've come back to the rubbish tip. Then I saw a shape big enough for me to understand. It was a tent. I went towards it and at once I fell over a dead man. He was wearing armour, but the birds had been at his face. There was another one near by, and then two or three . . . and not a sound, except for the kites and the flies.

I began to stumble around among the tents, spreading my pollution. It wasn't a job I much cared for, but the One God had chosen me to do it. I did find one man crawling along in his armour, but somehow I couldn't bring myself to curse him, so I wished him Peace and he groaned and fell dead at my feet. After a while I came to a road. I walked along it in the quiet sun until I came to what I thought was a cliff or a hill, but when I got nearer I saw it was the wall of the city, with a gate in it. Men in one of the towers cursed me and told me to go away.

"All the Assyrians are dead," I shouted. "I've polluted them! They're all dead!"

They cursed me again, but God gave me the strength to go on shouting until they understood what I was saying and their voices changed. They still wouldn't let me into the city, of course, but they sent a patrol out of the gate who told me to come back this way and they would follow a little way off on the other side of the road. I couldn't blame them, could I?

But you see what I mean about the odd way God works, and how confusing it can be at the time. Think of Him guiding Moses to make the Bronze Serpent, all those years ago, simply in order that a silly old man like me should become polluted and carry the pollution into the enemy camp and save the city! You might think it was simpler to strike the Assyrians down with thunderbolts, but that's not His way. He likes to work through people.

And people too—they can be very good, even to a poor old polluted outcast like me. The King gave orders that I should live here in this fort, and arranged for food to be sent out, and I'm really quite content. Though I do miss the Temple. And my poor old Bronze Serpent, and the people coming for wart-cures. As soon as things were back to anything like normal they started sneaking out here asking me to curse their neighbours for them, but of course I couldn't have that, and now they don't come at all.

I won't wish you luck with your sacrifice, in case just saying something like that makes it all go wrong. You'll have to tell them in the Temple that you've been talking to me, and they'll insist on a purification, but they're very good about it—they only charge a nominal fee. In fact they're very understanding all round. After all, I did save the city, didn't I? Thanks to the One God, of course.

Only I wish they hadn't melted the Bronze Serpent down. Then I could have had it out here and we could both have been polluted together and nobody would have minded. It seems a pity, after all these years. Moses made it, you know.

THE FALL OF THE CITY

*Told by an exiled Jew to an informal class of boys in Babylon. (That
same evening in another part of the town another Jew is telling the story
of the Creation at an open-air feast.) About 575 BC.*

◆

Remember Jerusalem!

No, I am not mad. I will make you remember Jerusalem, the city you have
never seen. I will build it in your minds, so that you can build it in your
children's minds, perfect, stone by stone, until a generation comes which will
build it again on the hill where God decreed that it should stand.

He punishes us a little while, a very little while, only a life-time or two,
perhaps. Then, when we are purified by sorrow for our old stupidities, He will
let us return and re-make a glory as great as Solomon ever knew.

Jerusalem cannot die. It is the hub of the wheel of things. It stands vertically
below the Throne where God sits in His heavenly city, and every stone of it
echoes a stone of that city and glows with the light of heaven, because God is in
it and sustains it also.

Do you ask me how such a city can fall? It cannot, while God sustains it. But
if He withdraws His presence, then fall it must, no matter how brave its
defenders, how high and thick its wall, how full its granaries.

We were there, your fathers and I. I stood with them on the ramparts. I
brandished my spear and shouted insults at the Babylonians, but my heart was
empty. That emptiness echoed another emptiness in another heart—from the
Holy of Holies, from the darkness between the great gold cherubim, God had
gone! This I felt, even then, as I yelled my curses at the Babylonian herald.

They came with a great army from the north. We had known for weeks of their preparations. We had laid the countryside bare and brought everything inside the walls. The streets were full of lowing cattle and the bedrooms bulged with corn-sacks. Then we shut the gates and waited. For a day and another day and a third the never-ending army crept up the Shechem Road—and still if you looked beyond the ridge you could see the dust-cloud of yet more regiments streaming away on the slow wind.

On the first day we stood, dry-mouthed, wondering when the assault would begin. A herald came to the gate and called on the city to surrender. We shook our spears at him and cursed him and his gods—but between insult and insult I saw, out of the corner of my eye, the glint of armour seeping like water along the hillside beyond the Kidron valley. That night their camp fires had reached the Bethany Road. By the third morning they had ringed us round.

And still the Babylonians poured up from Shechem, only now the procession was not of soldiers, but slaves dragging loaded sledges and oxen hauling baulks of timber, as though the Babylonians were coming not to destroy the city but to repair it. Soon we saw along the hillsides knots of men, some without armour, pointing or measuring or craning to study a scroll.

The slaves began to dig. Every day another tower sprang from the earth, and we watched the process like gardeners gazing at the first sudden seedlings of spring. The Babylonians ringed the city with their watch-towers and dug a rampart of earth between tower and tower and topped it with a palisade, and so we became a city within a city.

As soon as they had finished a rumour of hope spread along the ramparts and we crowded to the Northern Wall to watch them march away. Fools! Though company after company fell in along the Shechem Road, and the long brass horns snarled the signal to march throughout two whole days, when those companies had gone the army that was left still outnumbered all who were in the city, man, woman and child.

Then the most popular posts for sentry-duty changed. Our fool of a King, Zedekiah, had brought this destruction on us by intriguing with Egypt against his own sworn liege, Nebuchadrezzar of Babylon. Of course God had doomed the city to destruction long before, but that was the final brick which caused our house of folly to collapse with its own weight. Yet still men cajoled their officers that they might man the walls that looked towards Egypt, whence rescue could only come. They wanted to be the first to hear the silver trumpets of Egypt! Fools.

You see, we were the bait in a trap which the Babylonians had set. Nebuchadrezzar waited with his main armies up at Riblah. For month after month our besiegers saw to it that not one bag of meal seeped into the city, but it was strange how easily the King's messengers came and went. He would send a tablet saying, "Help us! Come now! The Babylonians have gone and left a weakened army behind. Strike now and you will be safe." A scroll would come back from Egypt full of praise and promises, but always saying, "Wait a little longer." Our fool of a King had learnt nothing, but perhaps the King of Egypt guessed why Nebuchadrezzar was lurking so patiently up at Riblah.

We began at last to starve. It is strange how long a city can survive after every last grain in the store-bins has been eaten. A year passed before that was true, and still the siege went on, month after month. Always there was a morsel to be scraped from here and another from there. Saddles make a sort of broth after you have eaten the mules. Many ate unclean things—God had withdrawn Himself, so why not? It is written that among the birds the kite is an abomination and shall not be eaten, and also the vulture, but I saw good Jews bait traps with scraps of horse-hide and catch the carrion bird that landed on one. We ate rats, of course, and dogs. I think if a pig had made its way into the Temple the priests would have declared it a mis-shapen lamb, and clean! Before the end, if a man died, I am not certain that all his scant flesh went with him to the grave.

By then few cared to man the walls that faced towards Egypt. We spent our time at the Temple, wailing to God to strike our enemies with a plague. We knew He had done it before, when Sennacherib had brought his Assyrians against the city in the time of Good King Hezekiah, but He sent no sign, except the steady plague deaths within the walls. *He* does not turn back from what He has begun.

At the beginning of the eighteenth month of the siege, at last the Babylonians moved to the attack, near the Ephraim Gate. We crawled along the ramparts and cursed them and dropped a spear or two—no arm was strong enough for throwing. They moved like builders at a storage barn, steadily and without confusion. They undermined a section of wall, levering the stones away, studying what they had done and starting anew. Oh, they were good engineers. When the wall was half undermined they propped it firm with the huge beams they had brought all those months before, and then worked again at the foundations as though we had not been there above them. A fall of mortar was more danger to them than we were.

At last they tied ropes to their timbers and stood clear. Long teams of slaves gathered to the ropes. The brass horns gave the signal, the slaves heaved and the timbers thundered clear.

Nothing happened. The wall stood as it always had been. A fluttering cheer rose along the ramparts, and I, even I, felt a sickly pulse of hope. Perhaps God had arranged all this long suffering to show us that He alone sustained the city. The wall stood by His will, and not by any strength that Solomon's masons had structured into it.

But before the cheering died I felt the paving of the walk-way tremble. The stones groaned. The straight line of the battlements wavered as if I were seeing them through a heat-haze. A long, low growl began, and thirty paces of battlement slid evenly down the slope below. The noise did not seem very loud, but it must have been heard—or the tremor of it felt—all through the city, because as the sound of tumbling masonry died and the dust-cloud smoked upwards I heard the wailing of women begin. I don't think it ever truly stopped until they led us away. Perhaps it is going on still.

An assault column came scrambling up the rubble with their shields over their heads. No need! A few of us stumbled towards them waving our spears, but the air was full of dust and a single cough was enough to tumble us to our knees, we were so weak. The Babylonians scarcely glanced at us as they formed up inside the walls and marched round to open the Ephraim Gate. I rose and staggered behind. I seemed to have dropped my spear. I was a child at a procession, tottering along to watch the pretty people.

The gates stood wide. Behind the arrogant horns, the chiefs of the Babylonians came striding in with their armour glittering and the flesh of their limbs so round and meaty that my mouth watered at the sight of it. We knew their names, having watched them all that time from afar—Nergalsharezar, Samgarnebo, Sarsechim the Rabsaris and the others. Behind them marched picked troops in parade order. *They* knew the fighting was over—though in truth it had never begun. I doubt if in all that siege ten men died of a weapon-wound!

Next the chiefs of the Babylonians had thrones brought and tables for their scribes, and they set up court by the Ephraim Gate and gave orders for the destruction of the city. Meanwhile our fool of a King was running away with his own picked guard. They got out through the little gate near the palace garden—I will show you in a moment exactly where it is set. They found a place in the tower-ring that was no longer guarded and fled towards the desert. Fled? Crawled, rather. They were so feeble, and even the King carried a burden on his shoulders. Contemptuously the Babylonians sent a troop to bring them back. The King was taken up to Riblah, where he was made to watch his sons being strangled before his eyes were put out. Then he was sent in chains to Babylon.

Our desolation moved more slowly. The Babylonians sacked the city as if they were on a military exercise, street by street, setting fire to all but the smallest hovels. Their slave-teams chewed away at the ramparts, section by section. The King's palace burnt for three days and nights. And the Temple, Solomon's Temple, the glory of the world, the knot that tied earth to heaven— that they smashed! Any of us strong enough to stand they whipped to the work. I myself hauled on one of the ropes which tumbled the great pillar Yakin that stood on the south side of the doorway of the house of God, but I did not tremble. God had withdrawn. It was no blasphemy. Not even when we broke down the roof of the Holy of Holies and let in the ragged daylight did I feel one tremor of His wrath. He was not there.

Only as my strength came slowly back on the endless stages of the march to Babylon did I begin to wonder. Where had He gone? Where was His Temple now, the seat of His holiness? I guessed at first that He would have chosen some mountain. Perhaps He had gone back to Sinai. Then I began to be afraid that he had found not a mountain but a city—and in the city a people—not us any longer, because of our long stupidities, but some other race now beginning on the test of worthiness which we had failed. Where?

One night as I lay in the desert between Damascus and Palmyra, I looked up at the stars and wondered whether among them God might have found a people wise enough to deserve His love. But as I was lying there, unable to tell star from star because of my tears, I heard a quiet voice speaking in my heart.

"I am here," it said. "You are still My people. I do not need a material city, or any Temple of hewn stone and timber, so long as My people carry the true city in their hearts. And I promise that one day stone will be gathered to stone and beam pegged to beam and My city will rise again. See to it!"

Next day I laughed and sang while we marched until my friends decided I had gone mad with sunstroke. But I shouted to them the words that God had spoken until they too laughed and sang.

Think now of those men laughing on the long and burning road. They were your very fathers!

That evening, as we sat and ate our ration, we made a sacrifice of part of it on a rough stone of the desert, just as Abraham might have done. There we vowed to God that when our sons were old enough to understand we would gather them into a school and teach them every wall and winding of the city we carry in our hearts. I was chosen to be the schoolmaster.

So today we begin, remembering always that it was God's will that the city should be destroyed. Only then could it be built—by you, or your children, or your children's children.

Now look. I have shaped the earth here into a long ridge. It runs north and south, with the Kidron Valley steep along the eastern side and the Valley of Hinnom joining it here at the south . . .

NOTES

SOURCES

The Old Testament received its present shape—that is to say the books which compose it were accepted as belonging together and having special authority—around 200 BC. These books in turn received *their* shape during the previous three hundred years, but especially in the Exile in Babylon from 587 to 538 BC. With the Temple destroyed and the people far from the homeland it had become vital to keep the tradition alive and to fill any gaps in it.

But these books were themselves put together from older books, which no longer exist. These are usually called sources. The three important ones for the early part of the Bible, as far as *Judges*, were probably written as follows: the one called J, in or soon after the reign of Solomon, say 900 BC; the one called E perhaps a hundred and fifty years later; and the one called P (from its special emphasis on priestly matters) later still, perhaps even during the Exile. The sources for the later historical books were court records, annals, legends preserved at particular shrines, priestly lore, legal case history and so on.

Stretching a long way back beyond even these sources was a whole tangle of traditions, a few written but mostly oral—folk-tales, songs, legends, treaties, proverbs and so on. Modern scholarship accepts that oral lore can be remarkably stable; though certain elements are changed to suit the needs of a new period, other elements—names, places, alliances of tribes, genealogies, the hard kernel of event round which a legend grew—these remain the same, even at the expense of making the whole story inconsistent with itself.

There is a lot of scholarly argument about sources—how old, how reliable, which source responsible for which passage. I have not paid much attention to any of this. Almost always I have told the story in its final form, even if it couldn't have reached that form at the time when my speaker is telling it. Where, as often happens, there are two versions of the same episode, I have used the one which seemed to me to make the better story, even where it is later or less probable.

THE FALL OF MAN

Genesis Chapters 2 and 3. The main strand of this story seems to have been written down in Jerusalem soon after the time of Solomon, about 900 BC. Many of the details (forbidden tree, angels or demons as sentries, etc) can be found in other ancient stories of creation, but there is nothing like this story as a whole. In the Bible there are two trees, one of knowledge and one of life, perhaps showing that two older versions have been woven together. The words in the English Bible—"the tree of knowledge of good and evil"—carry meanings which are not there in the Hebrew, where the phrase is just an idiomatic way of saying "knowledge of everything".

CAIN AND ABEL

Genesis Chapter 4. The mysterious "Mark of Cain" has always fascinated the romantic imagination; the explanation in my story is a possible one, a myth that remained after the custom it explained had died out. Thirty years ago many scholars went in for this sort of analysis, but there has since been a swing back towards believing that the original story-tellers may not have been as simple-minded as all that.

THE FLOOD

Genesis Chapters 6–9. The legend of a world-drowning flood is amazingly wide-spread, from Australia to the Arctic. The Bible story is an interweaving of two versions, one dating from about the time of Solomon and one from four hundred years later, during the exile in Babylon. There are close parallels with the story of Utnapishtim in the ancient Babylonian *Epic of Gilgamesh*, but these do not mean that either version was copied from the other. More likely they both stem from an even older Sumerian legend (in which the Gods decided to destroy mankind because the noise they made disturbed the Gods' sleep).

Sailors often used homing birds as navigational aids—if you were lost you could free a pigeon and get a rough fix on your home port from the direction it took. The pigeons, incidentally, come from the older strand of the Bible story and the raven from the later one.

BABEL

Genesis Chapter 11. Shinar meant Babylon, and the story may have some connection with the great ziggurat (a sort of stepped tower that represented the stairway to heaven) called Etemenanki. Still, it would be simple-minded to say this is just a story about Babylon. Its importance in the Old Testament is that it is the last story about God's dealings with mankind as a whole. From now on the focus narrows, and we seem to stare with a strange intensity at a single tribe of all the nations that spread out from Babel.

SODOM

Genesis Chapters 18 and 19. Like the Mark of Cain, the wickedness of Sodom has always fascinated certain minds. Nowadays it is assumed to have been sexual perversion, but this was not always the case. Isaiah writes as if the wickedness consisted in barbarous laws, and Ezekiel as though it had been oppression of the poor. One can make a good case that it was originally only the city-dweller's refusal to conform to desert standards of hospitality.

The story exists partly to explain the desolation of the Dead Sea plain (Lot's wife being an odd-shaped salt-pillar), but its main purpose is to ask Abraham's question why the just should be punished with the unjust.

The last bit of my narrator's dream refers to Lot's own daughters tricking him into incest so that they could have children and carry on the blood-line.

JACOB AT BETHEL

Genesis Chapters 28 and 22. Superficially these are two stories told to explain why (a) Bethel was a famous shrine, which it seems to have been even before Abraham came to Canaan, and (b) it became permissible to sacrifice an animal to God instead of one's first-born child. In other cultures in and around Canaan, child-sacrifice continued until quite late; it may occasionally have been practised (though this is disputed) among the Jews. The ritual killing of a child remained a very powerful and shocking act. To modern minds the killing of an animal to please a god seems shocking enough, but it was a central ritual in Temple worship.

The connection of Moriah with Jerusalem is very shadowy and late, but has become a widely held belief in both Jewish and Islamic faith.

REBEKAH AT THE WELL

Genesis Chapter 24. The Bible version is a perfect example of ancient story-telling (which was really not at all like my methods). It has great charm. Abraham had to send to his homeland for a wife for his son, to keep the blood-line pure. A desert well is usually just a crater with a path spiralling down to the water. Wells were great meeting-places.

JACOB AND ESAU

Genesis Chapter 27. To modern readers Jacob is a fascinating character—liar, coward, cheat, but still close to God in a more mystical and intense fashion than Abraham's down-to-earth companionship. (Isaac is a rather shadowy figure.) His other name was Israel, from which the usual Bible word for the Jews derives. (Or later writers invented a second name for him to account for the name of the race.) "Jew" comes from "Judah", and "Hebrew" probably from a word meaning wanderer.

JOSEPH AND HIS BRETHREN

Genesis Chapters 37 and 39–47. This famous story has layers of purposes and meanings. One is to explain the Twelve Tribes whose feuds and alliances make up much of Jewish history. The legend also explains the decline of the "Older-brother" tribes—Reuben, Simeon, Judah—and the rise of the two tribes named after the sons of Joseph—Ephraim and Manasseh. (There was a place for one extra tribe because Levi, the priestly tribe, had no territory.)

Then the presence of the Israelites in Egypt, long after God had promised them Canaan, had to be explained. (The Egyptians have left a lot of records, but none of them mentions the Israelites in Egypt.)

These and other meanings were knitted together into a story far longer than any other episode in the Old Testament, and cast into the form of the traditional folk-tale about the lucky youngest son who seeks his fortune in far lands and ends up as a prince, lording it over his cruel brothers.

MOSES AND THE PRINCESS

Exodus Chapter 2. The name Moses is probably Egyptian, meaning "begotten". It often occurs as a part of Egyptian names such as Tutmose.

THE BURNING BUSH

Exodus Chapters 3 and 4. The date of the escape from Egypt is disputed. A monument built by Pharaoh Meneptah in 1220 BC refers to a battle with the Israelites in Canaan, so it was before that. Rameses II (1290–1224 BC) and his father Seti I built a new capital on the Nile Delta, near the area supposed to have been occupied by the Israelites, and employed a class of near-slaves called *'Apiru*. This might be the same word as *Habiru*, which was used in many near-eastern languages for various groups of wandering outcasts—*Hebrew* derives from it.

Several mountains in the Sinai peninsula have been claimed as the Holy Mountain. The name of God consists of the Hebrew letters YHWH, pronounced Yahweh, but not normally spoken by pious Jews.

One way of reading this group of stories is to think of monotheism as being a simple, rigorous desert faith, which had been almost lost in the luxury of Egypt with its countless gods; the mission of Moses was to bring the Israelites back to the desert to discover the true faith. Some writers argue that the faith had been preserved among the Midianites, and that Moses himself learnt it from his father-in-law, Jethro, who is described as a priest of Midian.

THE PLAGUES OF EGYPT

Exodus Chapters 7–11. There has been a fashion for explaining the plagues as natural disasters—the bloody water was an infestation of red algae, the darkness was an eclipse, and so on. Sometimes such arguments are more unlikely than the story they try to explain—for instance, the idea that a civilisation as elaborate and lore-ridden as the Egyptian could be tricked by an eclipse is quite absurd.

Pharaoh's stubbornness about letting the Israelites go and worship in the desert may seem pig-headed, but there are Egyptian records about absenteeism in the labour-forces caused by the workmen going on sudden mass pilgrimages.

THE TWELFTH PLAGUE

Exodus Chapters 11–13. This episode is central to the Jewish faith. It acquired added importance during the Exile in Babylon (which was seen as a parallel experience) and the many persecutions since have renewed its impact, but it was central from the first. The earliest "Creed" preserved in the Bible concentrates on the rescue from Egypt as the proof of God's special favour to the Israelites (and makes no mention of the law-giving on Sinai).

It is thought that before the time of Moses two separate festivals were held, one involving the sacrifice of a lamb and one using bread baked without yeast ("leaven"), and that these were adapted into one Passover festival to commemorate the event. This is still held as a family feast every spring. The youngest child (as suggested in Exodus 13.8) asks questions about the meaning of the ritual and the head of the household explains.

The persecution of Antiochus led to the last great surge of Jewish nationalism, the Revolt of the Maccabees.

THE RED SEA

Exodus Chapter 14. I have followed the Bible account, with all the trimmings. Scholars looking for a historical kernel in the story (very few doubt that *something* happened) believe that the oldest strand contains the most natural details—the east wind, the bogging down of the chariots. Later strands are responsible for the more miraculous parts—the banked-up waters, the pillar of cloud. They also think that the crossing took place not on the Red Sea but on one of the marshy inland lakes which are now part of the Suez Canal. One can imagine a large group of runaway slaves trapped by their pursuers against a marsh and finding a seemingly miraculous pathway through. Perhaps their leader had already explored the area, and his exploit became part of the Moses story. The pursuers either lost their way or tried to take chariots along the secret path but sank through the marsh surface and were drowned.

THE SONG OF MIRIAM

Exodus Chapter 15. This is hardly a story. I have put it in because the song is thought to be a very old fragment indeed, close to the original event (whatever that was). Miriam was the sister of Moses.

SINAI

Exodus Chapters 19, 20 and 32. The Bible account of events on Sinai is extremely confusing. Several traditions and writers are involved, all using the episode to emphasise what mattered to them; if a rule had been "given on the mountain" it had enormous authority. But the episode was so holy that when these accounts were fitted together the men who did the work did not feel justified in leaving anything out. It had become holy too.

The part about the golden calf is a heavy reworking of an old legend. Some scholars argue that the Israelites worshipped Yahweh in the form of a bull for a long time after Sinai, and that the story was turned inside out to reach its present form. Most agree that the later reworking was intended to discredit the shrines which King Jeroboam set up after the Northern Tribes revolted from rule by the King at Jerusalem in 924 BC.

GIBEON

Joshua Chapter 9. A problem faced by the men who wrote the history of the conquest of Canaan was that they believed God had promised the land to the Israelites for their own exclusive use, but that even in the writers' time there were many other tribes still living there. With some of these—Gibeon especially —Israel had very ancient treaties. This legend—the one cheerful bit in the bloody history of the conquest —explains the treaty.

Gilgal was the great shrine of the Benjamin tribe. There were twelve standing stones there, one for each tribe, said to have been set up by Joshua to celebrate the first crossing of Jordan into the promised land. Jordan runs three hundred feet below sea level, so its ravine makes a natural boundary although it is not a big river.

JUDGE OVER ISRAEL

Judges Chapters 6 and 7. Between the reconquest of Canaan under Joshua and the choosing of the first King, Saul, by the last Judge, Samuel, the Bible lists the exploits of seven Major Judges, each time saying that they judged Israel for forty (or in one case eighty) years. It also lists five Minor Judges, with no exploits and varying lengths of rule. This makes it look as if the list of Minor Judges comes from an older and more historical document, while the Major Judges were originally tribal heroes whose exploits were later fitted into a scheme of rebellion from God, punishment by enemies, and rescue by a God-appointed Judge.

SAMSON AND DELILAH

Judges Chapters 13–16. The Samson stories are unlike anything else in the Bible, but like a lot of folktales. Samson is the hero-clown—the immensely strong, simple, practical-joking doer of deeds, fated to tragedy. One theory is this: the tribe of Dan first settled in the western foothills, but came under such pressure from the Philistines that they migrated to the north of Canaan. (Such a migration did take place.) In their new home tales of their struggles with the Philistines began to centre round one hero-figure, Samson, just as a number of British outlaw-stories clustered round Robin Hood. If Samson had been a British hero his legend would have reached us in ballad form (real Hebrew poetry was not like this at all). The big difference is that even the buffooneries of Samson had to be looked at through God-coloured spectacles. No effort has been spared to make them fit the main theme—but very few readers can have felt quite comfortable with the result.

THE CALLING OF SAMUEL

I Samuel Chapters 1–4. The life of Samuel was a turning-point. He was the last of the Judges, and as such he chose the first of the Kings. The authority of the long line of the Kings in Jerusalem stems from the point at which Samuel rejected Saul and anointed David. The famous picture of Samuel hearing the voice of God (by Reynolds) makes him too much of a child—he would have been almost a grown man. There is some evidence that the legend of his birth and dedication was originally told about Saul, whose name fits the Hebrew puns rather better.

Archaeologists have discovered that the great shrine at Shiloh was destroyed around this period and never rebuilt. The second part of the story probably comes from a lost *History of the Ark*, compiled at another shrine where the Ark was later kept. The Ark itself was a chest, with special carrying-poles. Later it was believed to contain the original Tablets of the Law, which Moses had brought from Sinai. It was considered to be the throne of God, and was held in great awe—almost as though it were radio-active, dangerous to go near, let alone touch, without proper ceremonies.

BETH SHEMESH

I Samuel Chapters 5 and 6. This also must come from the lost *History of the Ark*. The Philistines, being a confederation of city states each ruled by a prince, seem to have had greater cohesion than the tribes. This military advantage, added to by the Philistines' greater use of iron, eventually made it necessary for the tribes to unite under a King.

The loss of the Ark at Aphek has the ring of an historical event. Its return also is not improbable. A misfortune such as a plague could well be blamed on the presence of the Ark, and it would then be sent back to a place such as Kiriath Jearim, which though in tribal territory was under Philistine control. On the other hand, when the Ark was lost it could have been replaced, and a story would then be necessary to account for its return.

DAVID AND GOLIATH

II Samuel Chapters 17 and 18. In the Bible there are three conflicting accounts of how David came to be in the Israelite camp. There is also a brief reference later to a hero called Elhannan who killed the giant Goliath. The whole passage is one of the clearest places in which the interweaving of traditions can be seen.

Goliath may not have been a Philistine but a Trojan called Alyattes, who after the fall of Troy had come south to seek his fortune as a mercenary. His armour and weapons sound Homeric.

THE SICKNESS OF SAUL

I Samuel Chapters 18–26. David's successors were to reign in Jerusalem for the next four hundred years, so it was important to emphasise that his taking of the throne had been legitimate, and his apparent revolt against Saul not his fault. The story could be pure propaganda, but you have only to read the story in the Bible to be convinced that Saul's persecution of David did take place, in something like the manner described.

I don't know whether there were medical schools like the one I have imagined. The demons are complete inventions.

SAUL AT EN DOR

I Samuel Chapter 28. This is almost the only episode in the Bible in which magic plays a part. Such things must have gone on, because the prophets preached against them. The priestly oracle, which gave Saul no answer, was quite different. Perhaps it was not available to Saul after his massacre of the priestly city of Nob. It seems strange to us that this massacre was not one of the reasons given by the ghost of Samuel for God's rejection of Saul; in fact the chief reason was that Saul had failed to slaughter all the Amalekites after defeating them in battle.

ABSALOM

II Samuel Chapter 3—I Kings Chapter 2. This is a long passage known to Bible scholars as the Succession Document, which they believe to be a contemporary account of events at the court of David, later incorporated almost in its entirety into *Samuel* and *Kings*. The immediacy, drive and psychological insight of the Document make it unique among early histories (and not only in the Bible), though its purpose was to show that Solomon had come legitimately to his throne. Later writers, whose purpose was to prove the supremacy of Solomon's Temple over all other shrines, then used the Document to show how God, working through fallible men, brought the Temple-builder to power.

CITY OF GOLD

II Samuel Chapter 6, and I Kings Chapters 5–9. For the men who first shaped the books of the Old Testament, the building of the Temple was the summit. They were obsessed with the details of the Temple-building, and paid little attention to other aspects of Solomon's reign. It had to be glorious, so they barely mention that David's small empire was already beginning to crumble as the great powers to east and west gathered strength after a period of weakness. They tell us very little about Solomon. For "story" I've had to go back to the time of David and the extraordinary (and to us appalling) episode of Uzzah and the Ark, which presumably comes from the lost *History of the Ark*.

ELIJAH IN EXILE

I Kings Chapter 17. This section of *Kings* is mainly concerned with Elijah's, and then Elisha's struggle against King Ahab and his successors. There are three different kinds of prophets mentioned in the Bible: first, the colleges of ecstatic prophets, whom we met in the Babel story and the Choosing of Saul— these seem to have been associated with particular shrines; next the great solitary figures, such as Elijah and Elisha, who wrought wonders and spoke dooms to Princes; and finally the writing prophets such as Isaiah, who carried on this tradition in a new and more elaborate form.

Elijah was in exile because he had fled from King Ahab after prophesying the famine as a punishment for the introduction of Tyrian religious cults by the King's wife, Jezebel. Elijah's successor Elisha is also described as reviving a widow's dead son by very similar means. The assumption is that one story was copied from the other, but there is no way of telling which is the original.

ELIJAH AT CARMEL

II Kings Chapter 18. Two episodes may have become amalgamated here—a magical contest and a successful rain-making ritual. Baal was the Canaanite fertility God, and the Baals were local aspects of him, but these priests may have been worshippers of Queen Jezebel's imported Tyrian gods.

ELISHA AND THE BEARS

II Kings Chapter 2. This absurd little story has caused great embarrassment to commentators, who find it harder to account for than they do many far worse massacres and cruelties in the Bible. Until the last century there were indeed bears in the Mount Hermon range, but the last lions (smaller than the African breed) died out in the middle ages.

AT THE TOMB OF ELISHA

II Kings Chapters 2, 5 and 13. Some of the stories told about Elisha have an odd ring—like miracles attributed to some minor Cornish saint, trivial but engaging. Perhaps the Elijah stories were passed through his disciple Elisha, who saw to it that they were serious, but there was no one to do the same for Elisha himself. The dervish communities that tended to gather round such a figure would be hot-beds of credulous tales. On the other hand Naaman is an authentic Syrian name of the period, and the political set-up rings true, with the Northern Kingdom almost a vassal state of Syria. Naaman's disease would not have been true leprosy; other disfiguring ailments were called by the same name, though the ancients were aware of the difference. A true leper, however distinguished, would certainly have been expelled from the community.

ATHALIAH

II Kings Chapter 12. Athaliah was the daughter of Jezebel, so it is no surprise that she too was a formidable woman. Jehu in his rebellion managed to kill the Kings of both Kingdoms, so Athaliah used her powerful position as Queen Mother to usurp the throne of the Southern Kingdom—the only interruption in the line of descent from David of all the Kings of Judah. Of course there is no hint in the Bible of the twist I have given the story, that Joash might not be in that line at all. Joash was eventually murdered by two of his servants, and there is a strong suggestion in the parallel account in *Chronicles* that this was done at the instigation of the priests, perhaps because of his interference in their fraudulent handling of Temple dues.

THE BRONZE SERPENT

II Kings Chapter 18, v. 4 and Chapter 19, v. 35. This is the famous episode when, according to Byron's poem, "The Assyrian came down like a wolf on the fold," but their army was destroyed by plague. Hezekiah, in the eyes of the writers of *Kings*, was one of the few good rulers of Jerusalem, because of his Temple reforms and his abolition of heathen shrines. Along with these went a strong nationalistic spirit, which caused continual trouble with Assyria and

several near-disasters. Sennacherib, the Assyrian King, has left a record of the earlier siege which Hezekiah bought off by stripping the Temple of its treasure; at the same time the Southern Kingdom lost all its territory except the land round Jerusalem. In the British Museum is a series of marvellous carved stone reliefs showing Sennacherib's siege of Lachish—a vital Judean fortress city—in this campaign.

Of course there is no Assyrian record of one of their armies being wiped out by plague—it is not the kind of event kings inscribe on monuments. But the Greek historian Herodotus tells of an episode in roughly this time and area when an Assyrian army withdrew because mice nibbled through their bowstrings and the leather joints of their armour; this may be a misunderstanding; mice have a strong connection with plague (see the story about Beth Shemesh).

I have invented the link between the Bronze Serpent and the siege. This image probably had nothing to do with Moses but was a relic of some old Jerusalem cult which had become incorporated into Temple rituals.

THE FALL OF THE CITY

II Kings Chapter 25, Jeremiah Chapter 52, Ezekiel Chapter 12, v. 12, 13. Jerusalem was destroyed in 587 BC. Nebuchadrezzar had besieged and taken the city ten years earlier, and had then appointed Zedekiah King; so he treated this second campaign as the punishment of a rebellion, which is why the destruction was so thorough.

The nineteen-month siege by superior forces shows the strength of Jerusalem as a fortress.

The numbers deported to Babylon are a matter of dispute, but probably they included all the richer citizens, priests and craftsmen but not the peasant and labouring classes. The exile lasted fifty years, until Cyrus the Great took Babylon and gave the exiled Jews permission to return and rebuild Jerusalem.